Physical Cha
Bas.

(from The Kennel Club breed standard)

Tail: (Stern) well set on, rather long, strong at base, tapering, with moderate amount of coarse hair underneath. When moving, stern carried well up and curving gently, sabre-fashion, never curling or gay.

Size: Height: 33–38 cms (13–15 ins) at withers.

Body: Long and deep throughout length, breast bone prominent but chest neither narrow nor unduly deep; ribs well rounded and sprung, without flange, carried well back. Back rather broad; level; withers and quarters of approximately same height, though loins may arch slightly. Back from withers to inset of quarters not unduly long.

Hindquarters: Full of muscle and standing out well, giving an almost spherical effect when viewed from rear. Stifles well bent. Hocks well let down and slightly bent under but turn neither in nor out and just under body when standing naturally. Wrinkles of skin may appear between hock and foot, and at rear of joint a slight pouch resulting from looseness of skin.

Coat: Smooth, short and close without being too fine. Whole outline clean and free from feathering. Long haired, soft coat with feather highly undesirable.

Colour: Generally black, white and tan (tri-colour); lemon and white (bi-colour); but any recognised hound colour acceptable.

Feet: Massive, well knuckled up and padded. Forefeet may point straight ahead or be turned slightly outwards but in every case hound always stands perfectly true, weight being borne equally by toes with pads together so that feet would leave an imprint of a large hound and no unpadded areas in contact with ground.

Basset Hound

◇

Evelyn Elizabeth Lanyon

Table of Contents

PUBLISHED IN THE
UNITED KINGDOM BY:

INTERPET
P U B L I S H I N G

Vincent Lane, Dorking
Surrey RH4 3YX
England

ISBN 1-902389-50-6

82

Housebreaking and Training Your Basset Hound

by Charlotte Schwartz
Be informed about the importance of training your Basset Hound from the basics of housebreaking and understanding the development of a young dog to executing obedience commands (sit, stay, down, etc.).

Photography by Isabelle Francais
with additional photos by

Norvia Behling
TJ Calhoun
Carolina Biological Supply
Doskocil
T Fall
James Hayden-Yoav
James R Hayden, RBP
Carol Ann Johnson
Bill Jonas
Alice van Kempen

Dwight R Kuhn
Dr Dennis Kunkel
Mikki Pet Products
Phototake
Jean Claude Revy
Alice Roche
Dr Andrew Spielman
Alice van Kempen
C James Webb

Illustrations by Renée Low

109

Health Care of Your Basset Hound

Discover how to select a proper veterinary surgeon and care for your dog at all stages of life. Topics include vaccination scheduling, skin problems, dealing with external and internal parasites and the medical and behavioural conditions common to the breed.

142

Your Senior Basset Hound

Recognise the signs of an ageing dog, both behavioural and medical; implement a senior-care programme with your veterinary surgeon and become comfortable with making the final decisions and arrangements for your senior Basset Hound.

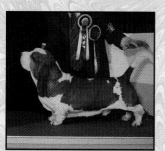

150

Showing Your Basset Hound

Experience the dog show world, including different types of shows and the making up of a champion. Go beyond the conformation ring to working trials and agility trials, etc.

Copyright © 2000 Animalia, Ltd.
Cover patent pending. Printed in Korea.

The publisher would like to thank the following owners for allowing their dogs to be photographed for this book:
Fred & Stella Atwater
Claude & N Hélène Déléage
Pascal Jocelyne
Camille Johnson
Alice Rand
Kay Rees
Mary Smyzer
Cynthia Wright

Mr George R Krehl's Basset Hounds Jupiter, Fino de Paris and Pallas, as they appeared in Cassell's *Illustrated Book of the Dog*, published in 1881.

The origin of the Basset, like most other hound breeds, cannot be positively traced; it certainly appears buried in antiquity. Figures found on the monument of Thothmus III, who reigned in Egypt more than 4000 years ago, are of dogs of long, low stature, the same proportions we see in the Basset Hound of today.

Similar figures were also found in early Assyrian dog sculptures. Dogs of similar Basset type but differing coat textures, one smooth, the other rough, were sent from Assyria to the Rhone district of western France between 125 and 200 AD. Writers describing these dogs told of their use as tracking and trailing traditional Basset game, the rabbit and the hare.

Onomasticon, a Greek dictionary in ten volumes, written by Iulius Pollux in the second century AD, mentions the dog being used by man for hunting purposes about 1300 BC. The ancient Greek author Xenophon made references in his writings of about 450 BC to small hounds used to hunt the hare on foot.

Early man hunted animals for survival itself, but down through the centuries hunting evolved from a means to sustain life into a

Zero, owned by HRH The Prince of Wales in the 1930s.

The modern Basset Hound represents generations of selective breeding for desired characteristics, all of which are abundantly evident in Ch Coombeglen Rufus.

sport. The landed gentry and nobility of France, as early as the 14th century, pursued blood sports as a social activity, using horses and large and small hounds, along with small terriers, in pursuit of deer, fox, badger and hare.

Selection for desired physical characteristics and mental traits to suit a purpose is how the various pure breeds came into being. In prehistoric times, the breeder was the caveman looking for a dog whose basic instincts were strong, and he used the best of these dogs to assist him in finding and catching food. Later, the breeder was the farmer, who found that keeping a game, hardy dog around helped keep meat on the family's table. The advantage to the common man was that the Basset was slower and could be easily followed on foot.

Later still, when the Basset was kept by the aristocracy, stockmen were employed and it was they who made the selection of stock. Having the wealth to do so, the aristocracy kept large

numbers of hounds together in packs. The terrain varied from district to district throughout France and so the desired type varied from pack to pack to best serve the challenges of the local hunt. This group of wealthy sportsmen usually followed the hounds on horseback.

Down through the ages, the breeder, whether he be the caveman, the farmer or the stockman, fixed type by repeatedly selecting for those desirable characteristics and traits known to suit the purpose at hand, and the long, low hounds eventually were refined and bred with some consistency.

During the Middle Ages in France, there were many varieties of hound described in early writings. How each of these

influenced the present-day Basset Hound is not clear. In the eighth century the 'Dog of Flanders' was called the St. Hubert Hound; St. Hubert was the patron saint of the monks at an abbey in the Ardennes. There were two varieties: a black-and-tan dog used for hunting boar and wolf, and a white variety later known as the Talbot Hound, a dog said to be 28 inches high.

Sir Thomas Cockraine in 1591 recommended that a dog known only as the 'heavy Southern-type hound' in southern France be bred with a Kibble Hound, the latter described as being of the broken and crook-legged Basset type.

Le Coulteux believed that all French hounds were derived from the St. Hubert Hound. He describes 12 different varieties of Basset said to exist around the time of the French Revolution (1789–1799). He felt that they were all related, having similarly shaped heads, long ears and dewlap. In another work dated 1879, there is mention of the Rostaing Bassets with long bodies and short crooked legs which were owned by a French marquis. This dog was described as having a grand Otterhound-type head with a rough coat and was probably of the type we know today as the *basset griffon* (such as the Griffon Nivernais, the Grand Basset Griffon Vendéen and

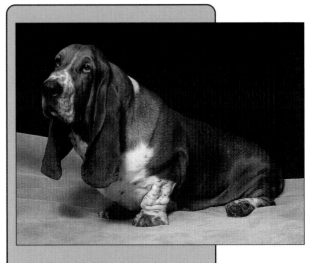

ACHONDROPLASTIC

You have read that the French word *basset* means 'low-set' and 'dwarf' but did you realise that today the Basset is known as an achondroplastic type of dog? Achondroplasia refers to a form of dwarfism primarily affecting the development of long bones, i.e. the limbs of young dogs. Growth in some areas is restricted or arrested, resulting in an animal normal in head and body development, but severely foreshortened in the limbs. The stunted bones, although lacking in length and frequently bowed, are strong, often stronger than those of normal legs. Dachshunds and Basset Hounds are typical achondroplastics. The rather short and anatomically deformed limbs, due to achondroplasia, equip the Basset specifically to enter rabbit warrens, badger lairs, etc., a task quite beyond hounds with 'normal' leg formation.

CANIS

Dogs and wolves are members of the genus *Canis*. Wolves are known scientifically as *Canis lupus* while dogs are known as *Canis domesticus*. Dogs and wolves are known to interbreed. The term *canine* derives from the Latin derived word *Canis*. The term dog has no scientific basis but has been used for thousands of years. The origin of the word dog has never been authoritatively ascertained.

the Griffon Fauve de Bretagne).

Sir Everett Millais, one of the earliest English breeders, theorised that the rickety-type Bloodhounds, descendants of the St. Hubert Hound, could have developed short, crooked legs. He believed that sportsmen who followed their hounds on foot selected specimens with the shortest legs, and the Basset Hound was the result of their continued selections.

In 1887 the prolific English writer, Stonehenge, wrote, 'In France, about twelve different breeds of hounds are met with, including the St. Hubert, the smooth hounds of La Vendée, the Brittany Red Hound, the grey St. Louis, the Gascony, the Normandy, the Saintogne, the Poitou, the Breese, the Vendée rough-coated hound, the Artois, and the little Basset, coupled with the Briquet. Of these, the grey St. Louis is almost extinct, and all the

This early drawing of French Bassets as they appeared in 1885 represents the two coat types, rough and smooth, which have been popular on the Continent for many years.

smooth coats, brave, and having double rows of teeth like wolves.'

Stonehenge further observed, 'In the many political storms that have swept over France, carrying away her monarchical pageantry and the impressing ceremonies of the chase, many of that country's ancient breeds became almost extinct. Among them, the basset-hound fared a little better than its blood neighbours—the hounds of others, with the exception of the Basset, may be grouped with the St. Hubert and the Red Hound of Brittany.' He goes on to say, 'The varieties of the Basset are innumerable, some being black-and-tan, and common throughout the Black Forest and Vosges, while the others are either tricoloured or blue mottled. The tricolour has lately been introduced into England in large numbers, having been first shown to the English visitors at the French show of 1863.'

Stonehenge uses the words of the earliest French authority, De Fouilloux, to describe the 'Basset d'Artois,' with which we are chiefly concerned. 'The Artesien, with full-crooked fore-legs,

Basset Hounds, when in proper physical condition, can leap hurdles and hold their own in agility trials. This action photo appeared in *Sport & General*.

PHYSICAL AND MENTAL

Since dogs have been inbred for centuries, their physical and mental characteristics are constantly being changed to suit man's desires for hunting, retrieving, scenting, guarding and warming their masters' laps. During the past 150 years, dogs have been judged according to physical characteristics as well as functional abilities. Few breeds can boast a genuine balance between physique, working ability and temperament.

Artois, Normandy, Gascony and Saintogne. Thanks to the sporting and patriotic instincts of the descendant of the old noblesse, Count le Couteulx de Canteleu, who spared neither trouble nor expense in his purpose, the smooth tricolour basset-hound of Artois has been preserved in all its purity. The breed was not revived; it had never died out, but it was necessary to search all over the "basset" districts to find, in sportsmen's kennels, the few true typical specimens, and to breed from them alone. In these efforts on behalf of the old breeds, he was greatly benefited by the valuable assistance of M Pierre Pichot, editor of the *Revue Britannique*. These are inseparably connected with the famous kennel of Chateau St. Martin, and hounds of Count Couteulx's strain are now as highly prized and eagerly sought for in England as in France. They are aptly described by the French writer De la Blanchere as "large hounds on short legs"'.

In Vero Shaw's 1881 *The Book of the Dog,* another of the earliest English Basset fanciers wrote, 'The Basset par excellence, though, is the beautiful smooth-coated tricolour of Artois, and this is the type with its rich and brilliant colouring of black, white, and golden tan, its noble Bloodhound-like head so full of solemn dignity, and long velvet-soft ears, the kind and pensive eye, the heavy folds of the throat, the strange fore-limbs, the quaint and medieval appearance...' This type, according to Mr Krehl, will always be associated with Count le Couteulx de Canteleu who set about to breed a line the Count described as, 'The head lays great stress upon the occipital protuberance...and is long, narrow and

The Wooton Basset Hounds were a well-known pack in the 1930s. Bassets were commonly used as pack dogs both in France and England during the first part of the 20th century.

thin in the muzzle, the ears very long; the head of the dog being much heavier and stronger than the bitch's. He gives about four inches for the height of the crooked legs. Colour, tricolour, sometimes ticked with black spots.' He goes on to say that, 'Some of them have more teeth than dogs usually have, and that many have a lower jaw a little shorter than the upper jaw.'

Also breeding about this same time, from much the same stock, were two other French breeders, Monsieurs Masson and Lane. Each developed a line, but with varying results. What happened in France in the 1880s also happens today. It is the selection of different traits that a breeder makes from his stock that form the easily recognised type known to come from a particular kennel. These three gentlemen were responsible for breeding Bassets, similar yet different in style, apparently easily recognised as the Fino de Paris type, the Termino or Masson type and the Lane type. Eventually the three lines were combined, each line needing attributes different from the others to keep the line healthy and breeding true.

It is interesting to note that these three types within the breed would have influence later on the type established in England and America. The two Couteulx types were defined as the Fino de Paris

FOLLOWING THE TRAIL
Aside from the Basset's big leather nose with large wide-open nostrils, there are several other breed characteristics that enhance his ability to follow a trail for hours and hours. The Basset's extremely long ears are velvety in texture and hang in loose folds, with the ends curling slightly inward. They are supposed to be long enough to fold well over the end of the nose. These ears, of course, touch the ground and stir up the scent on the trail. The skin over the whole head is loose, falling in distinct wrinkles over the brow when the head is lowered. The lips are pendulous, too, falling squarely in front and toward the back, in loose hanging flews. The dewlap is very pronounced. The excess skin around the head, muzzle and flews all collect the scent and hold it around the dog's knowing nose.

Lane type, while lighter still in colouring compared to the other two, was a very big, heavy Basset, with a large, coarse, domed head, decidedly lacking in Bloodhound-like expression, and ears that were long, broad and heavy, hung low.

Other important breeders during this period were Monsieurs Verrier, Machart, Gosselin, Hannoire and Baillet, and Col. de Champs. It is believed that it was from these gentlemen that the early stock was obtained and exported to England and America.

Wildfowler in 1879 wrote about the use of Basset Hound packs in the hunting of vermin. The Bassets' hunting behaviour was different from that of Beagle packs. While the Bassets were

This Basset Hound, well marked with extremely short legs, was owned by Queen Alexandra and named Sandringham Forester. type, a finer hound with rich colouring and a powerful physique, some with a flattish head with ears set high and small, with skull domed. The Termino (or Masson) type of Couteulx breeding had lighter colouring, the head was large and well shaped, good-sized ears hung low with well-developed flews and the nose was slightly Roman. The

These ladies mean business! While Greyhound racing was considered a gentleman's sport, Basset Hound racing was an outing for the ladies during the 1920s.

The Petit Basset Griffon Vendéen is the small French rough-coated Basset Hound that has become the most popular of the French Basset breeds.

part of a large group of dogs, each dog seemed to work on his own within the pack. Not easily aroused by the excitement of others, nor given to charging blindly after game, each dog preferred to investigate and make his or her own decisions about the importance of the trail and give tongue only when aroused to do so.

The Bassets were used on a variety of vermin, including the ferocious badger and the fox. They were also used for pheasant and woodcock shooting, and some were even trained to retrieve from water. Another interesting pursuit for the Bassets was the hunting of truffles, the great French delicacy, a potato-shaped fungi akin to the mushroom family. The Basset, with his great scenting ability,

located the underground site for the farmer and stood back while the truffle was excavated.

The Basset in 19th-century France was a smaller, lighter boned, more agile dog than the Bassets in England and America. The smooth-coated dogs were found in the Ardennes, Artois, Saintonge and Gascony regions, areas where the terrain consisted

Mr J W Practor's Basset bitch, Ch Queen of Geisha, shows the quality of champion dogs during the 1930s.

The Basset Artesian Normand is a French hunting dog that resembles the British dog but is lighter with a more conical head shape.

The Basset Fauve de Bretagne is a rough-coated Basset from France, designed to hunt on difficult terrain.

of open fields, farmlands and woods. The rough-coated griffon varieties went to the Brittany and Vendée regions where the countryside was rougher and the dogs needed more protection from the elements. By the mid-20th century, the varieties of Bassets were known as the Griffon Vendéen, the Artesien-Normand, the Fauve de Bretagne and the Bleu de Gascogne. The French kept these dogs primarily for their hunting abilities, rather than their companionship.

In the 1960s, the modern-day version of the Basset Hound, which had been developed and refined abroad, arrived in France and a club was formed in 1967. This is a distinct breed, despite its French origins in the 19th century, and registered simply as Basset Hounds.

It is interesting to note that the Fédéracion Internationale Cynologique (FCI), of which France is a member, considers the

Basset Hound, as we know it, to be an American breed, despite the fact that its roots are decidedly French. In France, the Basset Hound is simply one of 41 recognised scent hound breeds. The standard for the Basset Hound, which was adopted by the FCI, is the same as that of the American Kennel Club.

THE BASSET HOUND IN BRITAIN

In 1866 M Le Comte de Tournon presented several Bassets of the smooth-coated Artois variety to Lord Galway of Great Britain. Later these dogs were passed to Lord Onslow. Also from the Couteulx kennels came a dog named Model, imported by Sir Everett Millais in 1874, and he was the first Basset shown in Britain. In 1877 the Earl of Onslow imported Fino and Finette, also from Couteulx. Model was bred to Finette, and Sir Everett took a bitch puppy named Garrenne in lieu of a stud

fee. Later, in 1880, George Krehl imported Fino de Paris and these dogs and their progeny gave Britain its start in the breed.

The Basset Hound Club was founded in 1884, and in 1886 there were 120 entries at the Aquarium Show in London. About this time the differences in type among the British Bassets became obvious, and the two types of Couteulx hounds were in evidence. The 20 years of close breeding from the original French dogs had resulted in a finer, lighter dog than desired. Also, the dogs were not as vigorous as they once were, with a declining ability to resist disease (distemper in particular) as well as problems with reproduction, whelping and raising puppies. So in 1894 Sir Everett Millais took the matter in hand and crossed his Basset stud, Nicholas, by means of what we know today as artificial insemination, to the Bloodhound bitch named Inoculation. Dogs from these early crosses were bred back to the Bassets and the Basset's unique anatomy proved to be dominant. Within a few genera-

tions, it proved impossible to tell these crossbreds from pure-bred Bassets, and Sir Everett's strain was once again thriving. What we know today as 'hybrid vigour' was the desired result.

At the turn of the century, the Basset was gaining popularity and was firmly established in Britain. The first quarter of the 20th century saw a great deal of Basset breeding, including patronage from HRH Queen Alexandra who kept both rough and smooth hounds at her famous Sandringham kennels.

The Basset Hound Club had passed a rule 'that no unsound hound should be awarded a prize' at the shows. Then, as now, exhibitors complained about the poor quality of judging and that Bassets who were unsound in body, albeit with handsome Bloodhound-like heads, were winning. In 1910, feeling that the wrong message was being given to breeders, encouraging emphasis

A drawing by C Burton Barber, from the 1930s, of Sir John Everett Millais's Basset Hound, Model.

The smooth bitch, Sandringham Dido, was the property of Her Majesty Queen Alexandra, who fancied both smooths and roughs.

Major G Heseltine's pack of Basset Hounds was probably the finest Basset pack in the world at the turn of the 20th century.

on the head rather than the sound body and limbs necessary to hunt, the brothers Godfrey and Geoffrey Heseltine, breeders of the highly successful Walhampton pack, resigned their membership in the club. The Masters of Basset Hounds formed an association about this time. These fanciers kept hounds for hunting hare.

The Walhampton kennels were highly successful both in the field and in the show ring. To keep their pack strong, the Heseltines imported new stock from France on three occasions. The combining of their original British stock with the French imports produced a line sought after by others and a number of Walhampton dogs were exported to the United States. Walhampton came to an abrupt end with the untimely passing of the brothers

Heseltine in 1932.

Many established Basset breeders purchased dogs from the disbanding Walhampton kennels, including two prominent breed stalwarts, Mrs Elms (Reynalton) and Mrs Grew (Maybush). They combined Walhampton stock with their own and each continued successfully. The outbreak of the Second World War (1939–1945) brought most dog breeding to a standstill, with only 13 Bassets registered in 1939 and 7 registered in 1940. Mrs Elms and Mrs Grew somehow managed to breed a few litters through the war years, and thankfully both had quality stock at the war's end on which to base the next generations. By this time, however, both Mrs Elms and Mrs Grew were quite elderly and the reconstruction of the breed fell to Miss Peggy Keevil. The numbers of breeding animals available in Britain were so few that Miss Keevil imported three hounds from France between 1946 and 1951. The old and the new combined well and once again the breed was in sound shape. Miss Keevil's The Grims kennel was dominant both in the show ring and in the field during the 1950s and 1960s.

The Basset Hound Club had disbanded in 1921 due to the split of opinion between the show fanciers and the field and hunt members. However, in 1953, with the renewed interest in the breed following the war, the Basset Hound Club was reformed and Mrs Angela Hodson served as the first secretary. Mrs Hodson's foundation bitch came from The Grims kennels and produced many champions under her Rossingham prefix. Among the early supporters of the new club was a very elderly Mrs Grew. Another early member was George Johnston, who had owned some Reynalton hounds from Mrs Elm back in the late 1930s. Mr Johnston, and later his son, bred under the Sykemoor banner and were responsible for exporting foundation stock abroad. In 1959 Mr Johnston imported a young dog from France and, about the same time, the Basset Hound Club purchased an American-bred dog from the Lyn-Mar Acres kennels of Mrs Walton; both of these imports were useful outcrosses to the existing British stock.

THE BASSET HOUND IN THE UNITED STATES

The first mention of Basset Hounds in America is from the diary of none other than the first American President, George Washington (1732–1799). He wrote that his friend, Lafayette, sent some to the United States.

Almost a century later, in 1883, Lord Aylesford imported a pair for his ranch in Texas to be used for rabbit hunting. About this time, Mr Chamberlain

Two of the great scenthounds that share a common ancestor in the St. Hubert Hound, the Basset Hound (foreground) and the Bloodhound.

Interest grew slowly over the next three decades. To augment the stock already in America, both Erastus Tefft and Gerald Livingston imported numerous dogs from the highly successful British Walhampton line. These included the Walhampton pack leader, Walhampton Dainty, and English and American Champion Walhampton Andrew. Lewis Thompson imported English Champion Amir of Reynalton and Walhampton Nicety. Carl Smith imported two from France, Baillet's Trompette II and French Champion Baillet's Corvette (sometimes misspelled as 'Cornette'). Exhibition of Bassets at shows was sporadic during these early years.

purchased a Basset from Mr George Krehl for Mr Lawrence Timson of New Jersey. This dog, named Nemours, was the first Basset shown in the newly created classes for Basset Hounds at the famous Westminster Kennel Club show in New York in 1884. Nemours became the first American champion Basset Hound in 1886. The first Bassets registered with the American Kennel Club in 1885 were bred by Pottinger Dorsey of Maryland.

In the 1956 volume *The Modern Dog Encyclopedia* (edited by Henry P Davis and published in Pennsylvania), the authors sum up the differences between the French, British and American Basset Hounds, 'From this breeding has come the American Basset, a bit sounder in limb than the lighter French type and more compact and not so bulky as the English type, which was considered too large.'

In 1936 the Basset Hound Club of America was founded. The club held the first field trial in the US in 1937, and Hillcrest Peggy became the first Field Champion. In

Not quite the great packs of yore, these modern Basset Hounds still possess a strong desire to follow a trail.

1947 the first Bassets were exhibited in obedience trials with Walter and Marjorie Brandt's Lulu's Red becoming the first Basset to attain a Companion Dog degree. His litter brother, Lulu's Patches, became the second. Patches was also exhibited in the conformation ring and became a champion, as well as the first Basset to gain a Companion Dog Excellent degree, thus becoming the first Basset to hold all three titles.

By the 1960s the Basset was becoming very popular, and interest in the breed since then shows no signs of waning. The Basset Hound Club of America continues with a strong membership, and many regional Basset Hound clubs have sprung up in most states to further the best interests of the Basset Hound.

Heseltine's pack, the great Basset pack of Britain, as it appeared in 1912. These were fine working dogs that exhibited ideal type for structure, head and ears.

23

Characteristics of the
BASSET HOUND

We know that the reasons for the Basset's continued popularity are varied and due to the Basset being truly a versatile dog—one dog to fulfil many different roles. First and foremost, he was essentially a hunting dog of small game. Second, he was a specialist on hare, found abundantly on the Continent and in the British Isles, and cottontail rabbits, which are prolific in America. Third, his versatility as a hunter shone in that he could be used for grouse and pheasant and could learn to retrieve. He could be easily taught to tree and he makes a good dog on raccoon, opossum and squirrel. Last but not least, he was and still is today a steady, loving and affectionate family dog, making him a favourite as a household pet and companion for children.

All puppies are cute, but there is nothing quite so adorable as a Basset puppy—those soft, sad eyes framed by the long pendulous ears could melt a stone. With looks like that, it is almost impossible to turn a Basset puppy down, as he seems to be saying, 'Please, take me home!'

VIRTUES OF THE BASSET HOUND

The Basset is a breed that fits easily into most households. He wants to please those he loves and be in their company as much as possible, thriving on being with his special people. His tolerance level is extremely high, making him an ideal companion for children. He gets on well with other dogs and is tolerant of cats. He can be a good watchdog by virtue of his big deep bark, sounding an alarm to his family as well as deterring an unwelcome intruder.

Bassets are amenable to training but will never be the precision worker that the average Dobermann or Shetland Sheepdog easily becomes. The Basset's philosophy when you call for him is to reply, 'Yes, in a minute,' and carry on with what he's doing. Since the Basset likes to please, he learns what makes you happy and thus him comfortable, and will strive to maintain that status quo. He will be just as obedient as necessary to keep him on your good side but, being a Basset, he will think of some innovative tricks to keep you laughing and amused. Life with a Basset is always fun!

With his inherited desire to hunt and trail, and his body construction, he is an athletic and functional hound. Make no mistake, though; he will mature to be a good-sized dog. He needs a firm hand as a young dog so he doesn't jump on people when he gets older. He is not a lap dog although he thinks he is. He loves to go for long walks on lead, as well as runs through the woods or along the beach.

He is an easy keeper, too, requiring just the standard diet of quality dog food. One word of caution, though—Bassets tend to become fat due to owners who cannot resist the sad look that their dog gives them whenever the cupboard door opens. No dog benefits from excess weight, particularly one who is a big dog with a long back.

The Basset's nice short coat requires little grooming and does not moult very much if cared for regularly. He requires a bath occasionally and a weekly grooming, brushing and combing to keep the loose hair in check, and he needs his nails trimmed back.

The Basset's 'music' is exactly that, music to some but noise to others. A lonely Basset is going to howl, and in some urban settings

Yes, this photograph is in focus. It seems that this Basset's loose skin cannot keep up with his swift pace!

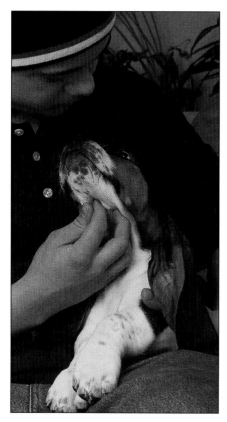

family car and watches television with him in the evenings.

A working couple also makes a good home for a Basset provided when they are at home that the dog is not left outside but is included, whenever possible, in the evening and weekend activities. He generally does well with children of all ages provided he has been raised with them, and the youngsters are kind, gentle and considerate of their dog. Children and dogs go together provided the child is aware that the dog is a 'person in a fur coat,' not a teddy bear or a doll.

Among the disadvantages, the Basset with his pendulous lips and ample flews can drool more than some other breeds that could be described as 'dry' (i.e. Basenjis, Borzoi, Whippets, etc.). If you are a fanatical housekeeper and cannot cope with some slobber on the floors, or even the walls, then the Basset is decidedly not the breed for you!

this does not make for good neighbour relations.

WHO IS THE IDEAL OWNER?

The Basset, due to his inherent easy and steady disposition, fits into most family situations. It doesn't take an overly dominant owner to become master of this dog, but the Basset, like almost every breed, needs to be a fully-fledged member of the household. He will do well with an owner who takes him for a long daily walk, includes him on trips in the

A few of the scent hounds, Bassets, Bloodhounds and Otterhounds for example, can have a certain, somewhat offensive, odour about them. The tendency to drool, along with all those folds of excess skin, are the main culprits, so the Basset is a breed that may require more bathing than his short hair would indicate.

WHAT DOES THE BASSET REQUIRE?

A household with someone home during the day is ideal for any dog, facilitating socialisation and housebreaking. In these modern times when so many couples work, and children are off at school, some planning must be done to accommodate the puppy while he is left alone. No puppy should be left loose in a house; even confined to the kitchen or pantry is not an ideal situation. A lonely puppy becomes a bored puppy, and quite soon damage is done to his surroundings. This is not good for the furnishings, nor is it good for the puppy, as many of these items when chewed and swallowed cause great harm and big veterinary bills. You will want to learn all about the proper use of a crate as a tool for training and housebreaking puppies.

The Basset's first instinct is to put his nose to the ground, sniff and follow that trail wherever it may take him; therefore, steps

DOGS, DOGS, GOOD FOR YOUR HEART!
People usually purchase dogs for companionship, but studies show that dogs can help to improve their owners' health and level of activity, as well as lower a human's risk of coronary heart disease. Without even realising it, when a person puts time into exercising, grooming and feeding a dog, he also puts more time into his own personal health care. Dog owners establish a more routine schedule for their dogs to follow, which can have positive effects on a human's health. Dogs also teach us patience, offer unconditional love and provide the joy of having a furry friend to pet!

must be taken to ensure he remains safe at all times. All dogs living in urban settings must have a fenced enclosure. No dog can be expected to stay within the confines of his own property nor safely run loose in a neighbour-hood, and Bassets are no

27

exception. Too many cars and lorries are going too fast to chance a dog being loose on the streets.

All walks must be on a collar and lead. Any time he is off lead he must be far away from traffic as his natural curiosity, his keen sense of smell and love of the chase will cause him to throw caution to the wind and just keep going, with or without his owner.

No dog wants to be shut away when the family is home. A

BY SCENT OR BY SIGHT

The Basset is a member of the Hound Group of dogs, which is divided into sight hounds (breeds that hunt by sight such as Afghan Hounds, Borzoi, Greyhounds, etc.) and scent hounds (breeds that hunt by scent such as Bassets, Beagles, Bloodhounds, Foxhounds, Otterhounds, etc.). The taller Bloodhound, rough-coated Otterhound and the shorter Basset with the long body share many breed characteristics especially on the headpiece.

SPAYING FEMALE PUPPIES

The advantage of spaying a bitch puppy before her first heat cycle (oestrous) is that the possibility of developing mammary cancer is greatly reduced. It is common for the first heat cycle to occur anytime after five months of age and is indicated by a swollen vulva and a bloody discharge. While previous thinking indicated a bitch should have one heat cycle before being spayed, that philosophy has now changed. Surgical sterilisation of puppies, male and females alike, is taking place earlier and earlier, and has been successfully done as early as six weeks of age.

Basset who is included, whenever possible, in family activities will be a happier, better adjusted dog.

BASSET HEALTH CONCERNS

Hypothyroidism (low thyroid function) is a fairly common health problem in all dogs, pure-bred and crossbred alike, and affects many older Bassets. Most dogs are born with normal thyroid function, but many become hypothyroid as they age. There are two causes of this condition, one being auto-immune thyroid disease and the other, more common, being idiopathic hypothyroidism.

The good news about the latter hypothyroidism is that the disease is easily diagnosed with a blood test, and treatment is easy

Bassets will be as lazy as you allow them to be. They need exercise, especially walking and playing with their owners, to stay in good physical condition.

KEEPING AN EYE ON THE EARS

Dogs, including Bassets, should be discouraged from riding in a car with their head hanging out the window as the rush of air is known to cause ear problems. Bassets obviously have pendulous ears and the ear leather covers the opening into the ear canal, making their ear canals a warm and moist haven for infections to begin. Early signs of ear problems are dogs who paw at their ears, constantly rub them on the carpeting, engage in a lot of head shaking and ear flapping, or have an offensive odour emanating from the ear canals. If your dog exhibits any of these symptoms, he should be checked by your veterinary surgeon. Early detection and vigorous treatment are desired in eliminating this recurring problem.

and inexpensive—simply a small pill taken once or twice daily. Common indicators of hypothyroidism are lethargy, tendency towards obesity, increased sensitivity to heat and cold, bilateral hair loss and bilateral blackening of skin, particularly on the abdomen and thighs. Hypothyroidism can also adversely affect reproduction.

Back problems in dogs are as common as they are in humans and Bassets are known to suffer from them as well. There are many reasons for dogs to have back problems (extending from the thoracic vertebrae through the lumbar vertebrae to the coccygeal vertebrae region) including familial as well as environmental causes. Dogs with skeletal problems that affect their

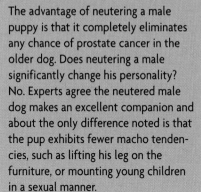

NEUTERING MALE PUPPIES

The advantage of neutering a male puppy is that it completely eliminates any chance of prostate cancer in the older dog. Does neutering a male significantly change his personality? No. Experts agree the neutered male dog makes an excellent companion and about the only difference noted is that the pup exhibits fewer macho tendencies, such as lifting his leg on the furniture, or mounting young children in a sexual manner.

flexibility and movement should not be used for breeding. Additionally, great care should be given to keeping your Basset slim and trim, with just a nice layer of fat and muscle covering the ribs. Ideally, he should look like a lean, hard athlete, capable of doing the job for which he was bred.

Common symptoms of back problems can be a reluctance to go up and down stairs or in and out of your car, shivering, hiding, lack of appetite and, in the extreme, hunched posture or partial or complete paralysis of the hindquarters. Any and all symptoms require immediate attention by a veterinary surgeon.

Defects in blood platelets was first reported in Bassets by J W Dodds in 1974, a condition known now as von Willebrand's disease. The little cells called blood platelets or thrombocytes normally form a first line of

defence against excessive bleeding whenever a blood vessel is ruptured. There are several abnormalities attributable to failure of the platelets to function as they should. In Bassets this defect causes bleeding from mucous membranes, and more severe bleeding after injuries or surgery. Careful pedigree analysis and blood testing by reputable breeders have reduced the incidence of this disease in dogs.

The Basset is also one of the breeds predisposed to the eye disease known as glaucoma. Like von Willebrand's disease, glaucoma is thought to be hereditary and, if not, it is certainly familial. No reputable breeder would be offended by your enquiry about incidence of these diseases within his line.

Paneosteitis has also been reported as occurring in young Bassets up to two years of age and results in what is known as wandering or transient lameness. Few veterinary surgeons are aware of its incidence in the Basset and misdiagnosis is common, often mistaking the cause for elbow or hip dysplasia, or patellar luxation. Definitive diagnosis is made by x-ray and it is recommended those films be reviewed by a radiologist specialist as the signs can be quite minimal and easily missed.

'Garbage can enteritis' is a common term given to dogs who indulge in eating things that are

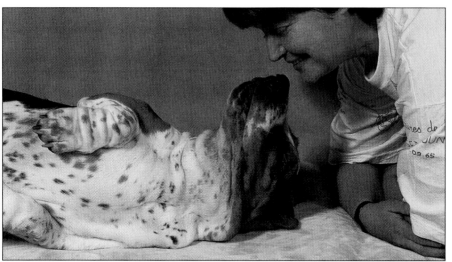

Love Basset style! There is nothing more important to a Basset than the love of his mistress (or master, as the case may be).

not found in their food bowl, resulting, of course, in gastrointestinal distress. Dogs who are known to have stolen from the kitchen table, raided the rubbish bin or pilfered from the laundry basket must be watched. The signs of distress would be lack of appetite, vomiting, diarrhoea or obstruction of the bowels. Please remember that puppies and adults alike are known to swallow items that are not radiodense, and a lady's nylon stocking or lingerie items will not show up on a radiograph but can cause total obstruction of the intestine. It is best to seek professional help as soon as distress is noted.

The Basset, like other deep-chested breeds such as the Greyhound, Irish Wolfhound, Saint Bernard, etc., is susceptible to gastric dilatation with torsion of the stomach, commonly called bloat. Early indicators of bloat would be lethargy, lack of appetite or a tight and/or distended abdomen. This problem can strike at any age and should be considered a true emergency requiring immediate action by a veterinary surgeon or the result is a quick and painful death.

THE BREEDERS HAVE IT!

Your children do not need to witness the miracle of birth by breeding their beloved pet. This knowledge can be gained by trips to the library, from books and videotapes. There are too many unwanted puppies in the world right now and unless your Basset is of top show potential and been specifically placed with you for breeding purposes, it is best to leave the breeding of Bassets to knowledgeable, committed breeders.

Breed Standard for the
BASSET HOUND

HOW TO ENTER A DOG SHOW

1. Obtain an entry form and show schedule from the Show Secretary.
2. Select the classes that you want to enter and complete the entry form.
3. Transfer your dog into your name at The Kennel Club. (Be sure that this matter is handled before entering.)
4. Find out how far in advance show entries must be made. Oftentimes it's more than a couple of months.

WHAT IS THE BREED STANDARD?

The standard is a description of the ideal dog, and in this case, the ideal Basset Hound. A standard is written for every recognised breed to serve as a word pattern by which dogs are judged at shows.

The dog show judge must have a picture of the ideal Basset firmly set in his mind's eye and when he sees such a dog he must quickly recognise the dog as the best before him. How a judge places the dogs in the class is based on how closely each dog resembles this written ideal.

The standard is full of terminology that is known within the canine world and is understood by judges, stockmen and breeders, but not necessarily by the pet-owning public. These terms are not always described correctly in a standard English dictionary but are found routinely in glossaries of breed books or general dog books.

Opposite page: The standard describes the desired characteristics of the breed by which Bassets are judged. The closer the Basset conforms to the standard, the better the chance the judge will select the dog for a ribbon.

THE KENNEL CLUB STANDARD FOR THE BASSET HOUND

General Appearance: Short-legged hound of considerable substance, well balanced, full of quality. A certain amount of loose skin desirable.

Characteristics: Tenacious hound of ancient lineage which hunts by scent, possessing a pack instinct, a deep melodious voice and capable of great endurance in the field.

Temperament: Placid, never aggressive or timid. Affectionate.

Head and Skull: Domed with some stop and occipital bone prominent; of medium width at brow and tapering slightly to muzzle; general appearance of

foreface lean not snipy. Top of muzzle nearly parallel with line from stop to occiput and not much longer than head from stop to occiput. There may be a moderate amount of wrinkle at brow and beside eyes. In any event skin of head loose enough as to wrinkle noticeably when drawn forward or when head is lowered. Flews of upper lip overlap lower substantially. Nose entirely black except in light-

coloured hounds when it may be brown or liver. Large and well opened nostrils may protrude a little beyond lips.

Eyes: Lozenge-shaped neither prominent nor too deep-set, dark but may shade to mid-brown in light-coloured hounds. Expression calm and serious. Red of lower lid appears, though not excessively. Light or yellow eye highly undesirable.

Ears: Set on low, just below line of eye. Long; reaching well beyond end of muzzle of correct length, but not excessively so. Narrow throughout their length and curling well inwards; very supple, fine and velvety in texture.

Mouth: Jaws strong, with a perfect, regular and complete scissor bite, i.e. upper teeth closely overlapping lower teeth and set square to the jaws.

Neck: Muscular, well arched and fairly long with pronounced but not exaggerated dewlap.

Forequarters: Shoulder blades well laid back; shoulders not heavy. Forelegs short, powerful and with great bone; elbows turning neither in nor out but fitting neatly against side. Upper forearm inclined slightly inwards, but not to such an extent as to

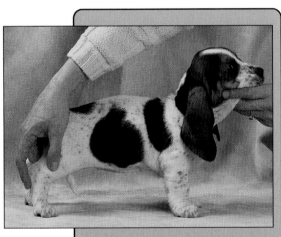

BREEDER'S BLUEPRINT

If you are considering breeding your bitch, it is very important that you are familiar with the breed standard. Reputable breeders breed with the intention of producing dogs that are as close as possible to the standard, and contribute to the advancement of the breed. Study the standard for both physical appearance and temperament, and make certain your bitch and your chosen stud dog measure up.

Undesirable body; high in the rear.

Correct front.

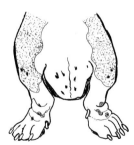

Incorrect front.

Too low on the leg.

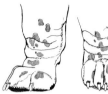

Undesirable foot, showing
nails too long;
weak pasterns and pads.

Correct foot.

Overweight.

Higher on the leg.

Undesirable ears.

Correct ears.

between hock and foot, and at rear
of joint a slight pouch resulting
from looseness of skin.

Feet: Massive, well knuckled up
and padded. Forefeet may point
straight ahead or be turned
slightly outwards but in every
case hound always stands
perfectly true, weight being borne
equally by toes with pads together
so that feet would leave an
imprint of a large hound and no
unpadded areas in contact with
ground.

prevent free action or to result in
legs touching each other when
standing or in action; forechest
fitting neatly into crook when
viewed from front. Knuckling-
over highly undesirable. Wrinkles
of skin on lower legs.

Tail: (Stern) well set on, rather
long, strong at base, tapering, with
moderate amount of coarse hair

Body: Long and deep throughout
length, breast bone prominent but
chest neither narrow nor unduly
deep; ribs well rounded and
sprung, without flange, carried
well back. Back rather broad;
level; withers and quarters of
approximately same height,
though loins may arch slightly.
Back from withers to inset of
quarters not unduly long.

Hindquarters: Full of muscle and
standing out well, giving an
almost spherical effect when
viewed from rear. Stifles well
bent. Hocks well let down and
slightly bent under but turn
neither in nor out and just under
body when standing naturally.
Wrinkles of skin may appear

underneath. When moving, stern carried well up and curving gently, sabre-fashion, never curling or gay.

Gait/Movement: Most important. Smooth free action with forelegs reaching well forward and hind legs showing powerful thrust, hound moving true both front and rear. Hocks and stifles never stiff in movement, nor must any toes be dragged.

Coat: Smooth, short and close without being too fine. Whole outline clean and free from feathering. Long haired, soft coat with feather highly undesirable.

Colour: Generally black, white and tan (tri-colour); lemon and

THE IDEAL SPECIMEN

According to The Kennel Club, 'The Breed Standard is the "Blueprint" of the ideal specimen in each breed approved by a governing body, e.g., The Kennel Club, the Fédération Cynologique International (FCI) and the American Kennel Club.

'The Kennel Club writes and revises Breed Standards taking account of the advice of Breed Councils/Clubs. Breed Standards are not changed lightly to avoid "changing the standard to fit the current dogs" and the health and well being of future dogs is always taken into account when new standards are prepared or existing ones altered.'

DID YOU KNOW?

A well-proportioned Basset is said to be built in a four-to-three ratio—the height at the withers is approximately three-fourths of the measurement from withers to tail. While the Basset Hound standard describes the 'Back from withers to inset of quarters not unduly long,' no actual measurements are given other than the height, which from ground to withers should be 33–38 cms (13–15 ins.)

white (bi-colour); but any recognised hound colour acceptable.

Size: Height: 33–38 cms (13–15 ins) at withers.

Faults: Any departure from the foregoing points should be considered a fault and the seriousness with which the fault should be regarded should be in exact proportion to its degree.

Note: Male animals should have two apparently normal testicles fully descended into the scrotum.

ARE YOU A BASSET PERSON?

The Basset Hound requires an owner who can be the boss of the relationship, gently but firmly explaining the rules of the house, and enforcing them despite that sad forlorn look his devoted dog gives him.

The Basset is a big dog on short legs, and while he's growing up he has plenty of energy as any youngster does. He can be charming, engaging, affectionate, yet mischievous and adventurous. He requires a great deal of your time from purchase throughout his puppyhood, into his adolescent days, until he reaches maturity and becomes a responsible canine citizen. Do you have the time for the most basic of daily care, a walk, no matter the weather? As a puppy your Basset should never be given too much exercise because of the heavy-boned front but as an adult, he will benefit from moderate exercise and look forward to his daily walk with you. Your Basset will require a degree of commitment and care all of his life, possibly as long as

12 to 15 years in length. Are you ready to devote the time your Basset needs and deserves? If you don't have the time or the willingness to make time, then please don't choose a Basset as a companion.

Space is another important consideration as, after all, that puppy is going to grow up into a dog of fair size. The Basset in early puppyhood may be well accommodated in a corner of your kitchen but after only a few months a larger space will be required. A garden with a fence

DO YOUR HOMEWORK!

In order to know whether or not a puppy will fit into your lifestyle, you need to assess his personality. A good way to do this is to interact with his parents. Your pup inherits not only his appearance but also his person-ality and temperament from the sire and dam. If the parents are fearful or overly aggressive, these same traits may likely show up in your puppy.

is a basic and reasonable expectation. Care must be taken to protect your puppy's heavy-boned front assembly by ensuring he doesn't jump off anything, the chesterfield, stairs, tables, etc. A good rule of thumb is never lift him onto anything that he cannot jump onto himself.

In addition, there are the usual problems associated with puppies of any breed like the damage likely to be sustained by your floors, furniture, flowers and, not least of all, to your freedom (of movement) when planning a holiday or weekend trips. This union is a serious affair and should be deeply considered, but once decided, your choice of a Basset can be the most rewarding of all breeds. A few suggestions will help in the purchase of your dog.

PURCHASING THE BASSET PUPPY

Most likely you are seeking a pet Basset, not necessarily a show dog. That does not mean that you are looking for a second-rate model. A 'pet-quality' Basset is not like a second-hand car or a 'slightly irregular' suit jacket. Your pet must be as sound, healthy and temperamentally fit as any top show dog. Pet owners do not want a Basset who can't run smoothly and easily, who is not trustworthy and reliable

OWNERSHIP RESPONSIBILITY
Unfortunately, when a puppy is bought by someone who does not take into consideration the time and attention that dog ownership requires, it is the puppy who suffers when he is either abandoned or placed in a shelter by a frustrated owner. So all of the 'homework' you do in preparation for your pup's arrival will benefit you both. The more informed you are, the more you will know what to expect and the better equipped you will be to handle the ups and downs of raising a puppy. Hopefully, everyone in the household is willing to do his part in raising and caring for the pup. The anticipation of owning a dog often brings a lot of promises from excited family members: 'I will walk him every day,' 'I will feed him,' 'I will housebreak him,' etc., but these things take time and effort, and promises can easily be forgotten once the novelty of the new pet has worn off.

The safest method of obtaining your new Basset puppy is to seek out a reputable breeder. This is suggested even if you are not looking for a show specimen. The novice breeders and pet owners who advertise at attractive prices in the local newspapers are probably kind enough toward their dogs, but perhaps do not have the expertise or facilities required to successfully raise these animals. These pet puppies are frequently incorrectly weaned and left with the mother too long without the supplemental feeding required by this breed. This lack of proper feeding can cause indigestion, rickets, weak bones, poor teeth and other problems. Veterinary bills may soon distort initial savings into financial, or worse, emotional loss.

around children and strangers or who does not look like a Basset. You are not buying a black-and-tan toy dog or a lanky shaggy dog; you want a Basset: a handsome hound with a lovely head and a soulful expression, soundly built with good eyes and a loveable personality. If these qualities are not important to you as a Basset owner, then you should go to the shelter and rescue any healthy appealing mongrel.

Enquire about inoculations and when the puppy was last checked for worms. Check the ears for any signs of mites or irritation. Are the eyes clear and free of any debris? The puppy

When faced with the selection of a Basset puppy from a large litter, you may require assistance. More important than colour and colour pattern are health and temperament.

coat is softer than the adult coat. Look for expression in your puppy's eyes, as this is a good sign of intelligence. The look of the Basset is always soft, sad and soulful.

Note the way your choice moves. The Basset, even in puppyhood, should show sound, deliberate movement with no tendency to stumble or drag his hind feet. Do not mistake a little puppy awkwardness for a physical defect. Look at the mouth to make sure that the bite is fairly even, although maturity can often correct errors present at puppyhood.

If you have any doubts, ask to see the parents' mouths. This brings up an important point— do not purchase a puppy without first seeing at least one of the parents.

DID YOU KNOW?
You should not even think about buying a puppy that looks sick, undernourished, overly frightened or nervous. Sometimes a timid puppy will warm up to you after a 30-minute 'let's-get-acquainted' session.

WHERE TO BEGIN?

If you are convinced that the Basset is the ideal dog for you, it's time to learn about where to find a puppy and what to look for. Locating a litter of Bassets should not present a problem for the new owner. You should enquire about breeders in your area who enjoy a good reputation in the breed. You are looking for an established breeder with outstanding dog ethics and a strong commitment to the breed. New owners should have as many questions as they have

doubts. An established breeder is indeed the one to answer your four million questions and make you comfortable with your choice of the Basset Hound. An established breeder will sell you a puppy at a fair price if, and only if, the breeder determines that you are a suitable, worthy owner of his/her dogs. An established breeder can be relied upon for advice, no matter what time of day or night. A reputable breeder will accept a puppy back, without questions, should

DOCUMENTATION

Two important documents you will get from the breeder are the pup's pedigree and registration certificate. The breeder should register the litter and each pup with The Kennel Club, and it is necessary for you to have the paperwork if you plan on showing or breeding in the future.

Make sure you know the breeder's intentions on which type of registration he will obtain for the pup. There are limited registrations which may prohibit the dog from being shown, bred or from competing in non-confor-mation trials such as Working or Agility if the breeder feels that the pup is not of sufficient quality to do so. There is also a type of registration that will permit the dog in non-conforma-tion competition only.

On the reverse side of the registration certificate, the new owner can find the transfer section which must be signed by the breeder.

champions and working lines. The real quality breeders are quiet and unassuming. You hear about them at the shows and trials, by word of mouth. You may be well advised to avoid the novice who lives only a couple of miles away. The local novice breeder, trying so hard to get rid of that first litter of puppies, is more than accommodating and anxious to sell you one. That breeder will charge you as much as any established breeder. The novice breeder isn't going to interrogate you and your family about your intentions with the puppy, the environment and training you can provide, etc. That breeder will be nowhere to be found when your poorly bred, badly adjusted four-pawed monster starts to growl and spit up at midnight or eat the family cat!

Choosing a breeder is an important first step in dog ownership. Fortunately, the majority of Basset breeders are devoted to the breed and its well-being. New owners should have little problem finding a reputable breeder who doesn't live on the other side of the country (or in a different country). The Kennel Club is able to recommend breeders of quality Bassets, as can any local all-breed club or Basset club. Don't forget to discuss health problems with the breeder: what

you decide that this is not the right dog for you.

When choosing a breeder, reputation is much more important than convenience of location. Do not be overly impressed by breeders who run brag advertisements in the presses about their stupendous are his experiences with back problems, glaucoma, hypothroidism, etc.

Potential owners are encouraged to attend dog shows and field trials to see the Bassets in action, to meet owners and handlers firsthand and to get an idea what Bassets look like outside a photographer's lens. Provided you approach the handlers when they are not terribly busy with the dogs, most are more than willing to answer questions, recommend breeders and give advice.

Now that you have contacted and met a breeder or two and made your choice about which breeder is best suited to your needs, it's time to visit the litter. Keep in mind that many top breeders have waiting lists. Sometimes new owners have to

DID YOU KNOW?
Breeders rarely release puppies until they are eight to ten weeks of age. This is an acceptable age for most breeds of dog, excepting toy breeds, which are not released until around 12 weeks, given their petite sizes. If a breeder has a puppy that is 12 weeks or more, it is likely well socialised and housetrained. Be sure that it is otherwise healthy before deciding to take it home.

INSURANCE
Many good breeders will offer you insurance with your new puppy, which is an excellent idea. The first few weeks of insurance will probably be covered free of charge or with only minimal cost, allowing you to take up the policy when this expires. If you own a pet dog, it is sensible to take out such a policy as veterinary fees can be high, although routine vaccinations and boosters are not covered. Look carefully at the many options open to you before deciding which suits you best.

wait as long as two years for a puppy. If you are really committed to the breeder whom you've selected, then you will wait (and hope for an early arrival!). If not, you may have to resort to your second or third choice breeder. Don't be too anxious, however. If the breeder doesn't have any waiting list, or any customers, there is probably a good reason. It's no different than visiting a pub with no clientele. The better pubs and restaurants always have a

waiting list—and it's usually worth the wait. Besides, isn't a puppy more important than a pint?

Since you are likely choosing a Basset as a pet dog and not a working dog, you simply should select a pup that is friendly and attractive. Bassets generally have large litters, with 15 puppies not an uncommon number, so selection is good once you have located a desirable litter. While the basic structure of the breed has little variation, beware of the shy or overly aggressive puppy: be especially conscious of the nervous Basset pup. Don't let sentiment or emotion trap you into buying the runt of the litter.

The gender of your puppy is largely a matter of personal taste, although there is a common belief among those who breed Bassets that bitches are quicker to learn and generally more loving and faithful. Males learn more slowly but retain the lesson longer. The difference in size is noticeable but slight. Coloration is not a grave concern with this breed, and all the hound patterns are attractive and eye-catching.

Breeders commonly allow visitors to see the litter by around the fifth or sixth week, and puppies leave for their new homes between the eighth and tenth week. Breeders who permit their puppies to leave early are more interested in your pounds than their puppies' well being. Puppies need to learn the rules of the trade from their dams, and most dams continue teaching the pups manners, and dos and don'ts until around the eighth week. Breeders spend significant amounts of time with the Basset toddlers so that they are able to interact with the 'other species,' i.e. humans. Given the long history that dogs and humans have, bonding between the two species is natural but must be nurtured. A well-bred, well-socialised Basset pup wants to be near you and please you.

COMMITMENT OF OWNERSHIP

After considering all of these factors, you have most likely already made some very important decisions about selecting your puppy. You have chosen a Basset, which means that you have decided which characteristics you want in a dog and what type of dog will best fit into your family and lifestyle. If you have selected a breeder, you have gone a step further—you have done your research and found a responsible, conscientious person who breeds quality Bassets and who should be a reliable source of help as you and your puppy adjust to life together. If you have observed a litter in action, you have obtained a firsthand look at the dynamics of a puppy 'pack' and, thus, you have become familiar with each pup's individual personality—perhaps you have even found one that particularly appeals to you.

However, even if you have not yet found the Basset puppy of your dreams, observing pups will help you learn to recognise certain behaviour and to determine what a pup's behaviour indicates about his temperament. You will be able to pick out which pups are the leaders, which ones are less outgoing, which ones are confident, which ones are shy,

YOUR SCHEDULE . . .

If you lead an erratic, unpredictable life, with daily or weekly changes in your work requirements, consider the problems of owning a puppy. The new puppy has to be fed regularly, socialised (loved, petted, handled, introduced to other people) and, most importantly, allowed to visit outdoors for toilet training. As the dog gets older, it can be more tolerant of deviations in its feeding and toilet relief.

PUPPY APPEARANCE

Your puppy should have a well-fed appearance but not a distended abdomen, which may indicate intestinal parasites (commonly called worms) or incorrect feeding, or both. The body should be firm, with a solid feel. The skin of the abdomen should be pale pink and clean, without signs of scratching or rash. It is always a good idea to take a fresh stool sample to the veterinary surgeon for microscopic analysis. If you can't take the sample immediately to the veterinary office then put it in an enclosed container and store it in the refrigerator. If parasites are present then the correct medication can be dispensed.

on the way to dog ownership. It may seem like a lot of effort… and you have not even taken the pup home yet! Remember, though, you cannot be too careful when it comes to deciding on the type of dog you want and finding out about your prospective pup's background. Buying a puppy is not—or should not be—just another whimsical purchase. This is one instance in which you actually do get to choose your own family! You may be thinking that buying a puppy should be fun—it should not be so serious and so much work. Keep in mind that your puppy is not a cuddly stuffed toy or decorative lawn ornament, but a creature that will become a real member of your family. You will come to realise that, while buying a puppy is a pleasurable and exciting endeavour, it is not something to be taken lightly. Relax…the fun will start when the pup comes home!

Always keep in mind that a

playful, friendly, aggressive, etc. Equally as important, you will learn to recognise what a healthy pup should look and act like. All of these things will help you in your search, and when you find the Basset that was meant for you, you will know it!

Researching your breed, selecting a responsible breeder and observing as many pups as possible are all important steps

QUALITY FOOD

The cost of food must also be mentioned. All dogs need a good quality food with an adequate supply of protein to develop their bones and muscles properly. Most dogs are not picky eaters but unless fed properly they can quickly succumb to skin problems.

puppy is nothing more than a baby in a furry disguise…a baby who is virtually helpless in a human world and who trusts his owner for fulfilment of his basic needs for survival. In addition to water and shelter, your pup needs care, protection, guidance and love. If you are not prepared to commit to this, then you are not prepared to own a dog.

Wait a minute, you say. How hard could this be? All of my neighbours own dogs and they seem to be doing just fine. Why should I have to worry about all of this? Well, you should not worry about it; in fact, you will probably find that once your Basset pup gets used to his new home, he will fall into his place in the family quite naturally. But it never hurts to emphasise the commitment of dog ownership. With some time and patience, it is really not too difficult to raise a curious and exuberant Basset pup to be a well-adjusted and well-mannered adult dog—a dog that could be your most loyal friend.

PREPARING PUPPY'S PLACE IN YOUR HOME

Researching your breed and finding a breeder are only two aspects of the 'homework' you will have to do before bringing your Basset puppy home. You will also have to prepare your home and family for the new

> **BOY OR GIRL?**
> Another important consideration remains to be discussed and that is the sex of your puppy. The personality differences between a male and a bitch are infinitesimal. The sex of the Basset you choose as a pet really doesn't matter since, unless you are embarking on the path to becoming a responsible breeder of quality Bassets, you will be neutering the male or spaying the bitch. The world has too many unwanted dogs now so neutering all but the very best of show and breeding stock is the responsible thing to do.

addition. Just as you would prepare a nursery for a newborn baby, you will need to designate a place in your home that will be the puppy's own. How you prepare your home will depend on how much freedom the dog will be allowed. Whatever you decide, you must ensure that he has a place that he can 'call his own.'

When you bring your new puppy into your home, you are bringing him into what will become his home as well. Obviously, you did not buy a puppy so that he could take over your house, but in order for a puppy to grow into a stable, well-adjusted dog, he has to feel comfortable in his surroundings. Remember, he is leaving the

PUPPY PERSONALITY

When a litter becomes available to you, choosing a pup out of all those adorable faces will not be an easy task! Sound temperament is of utmost importance, but each pup has its own personality and some may be better suited to you than others. A feisty, independent pup will do well in a home with older children and adults, while quiet, shy puppies will thrive in a home with minimum noise and distractions. Your breeder knows the pups best and should be able to guide you in the right direction.

warmth and security of his mother and littermates, as well as the familiarity of the only place he has ever known, so it is important to make his transition as easy as possible. By preparing a place in your home for the puppy, you are making him feel as welcome as possible in a strange new place. It should not take him long to get used to it, but the sudden shock of being transplanted is somewhat traumatic for a young pup. Imagine how a small child would feel in the same situation—that is how your puppy must be feeling. It is up to you to reassure him and to let him know, 'Little chap, you are going to like it here!'

WHAT YOU SHOULD BUY

CRATE

To someone unfamiliar with the use of crates in dog training, it may seem like punishment to shut a dog in a crate, but this is not the case at all. Although all breeders do not advocate crate training, more and more breeders and trainers are recommending crates as preferred tools for pet puppies as well as show puppies. Crates are not cruel—crates have many humane and highly effective uses in dog care and training. For example, crate training is a very popular and very successful housebreaking method. A crate can keep your dog safe during travel; and, perhaps most importantly, a crate provides your dog with a place of his own in your home. It serves as a 'doggie bedroom' of sorts—your Basset can curl up in his crate when he wants to sleep or when he just needs a break. Many dogs sleep in their crates overnight. With soft bedding and a favourite toy, a crate becomes a cosy pseudo-den for your dog. Like his ancestors, he too will seek out the comfort and retreat of a den—you just happen to be providing him with something a little more luxurious than his early ancestors enjoyed.

As far as purchasing a crate, the type that you buy is up to you. It will most likely be one of the two most popular types: wire or fibreglass. There are advantages and disadvantages to each type. For example, a wire crate is more open, allowing the air to flow through and affording the dog a view of what is going on around him while a fibreglass crate is sturdier. Both can double as travel crates, providing protection for the dog. The size of the crate is another thing to consider. Puppies do not stay puppies forever—in fact, sometimes it seems as if they grow right before your eyes. A small-sized crate may be fine for a very young Basset pup, but it will not do him much good for long! Unless

'YOU BETTER SHOP AROUND!'
Finding a reputable breeder that sells healthy pups is very important, but make sure that the breeder you choose is not only someone you respect but also with whom you feel comfortable. Your breeder will be a resource long after you buy your puppy, and you must be able to call with reasonable questions without being made to feel like a pest! If you don't connect on a personal level, investigate some other breeders before making a final decision.

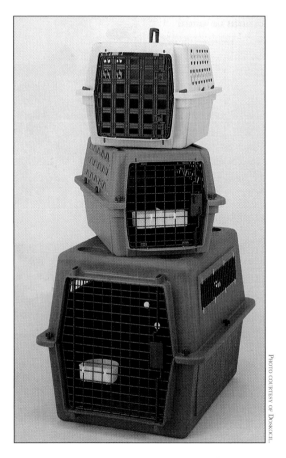

PHOTO COURTESY OF DOSKOCIL.

BEDDING

Veterinary bedding in the dog's crate will help the dog feel more at home and you may also like to pop in a small blanket. This will take the place of the leaves, twigs, etc., that the pup would use in the wild to make a den; the pup can make his own 'burrow' in the crate. Although your pup is far removed from his den-making ancestors, the denning instinct is still a part of his genetic makeup. Second, until you bring your pup home, he has been sleeping amidst the warmth of his mother and litter-mates, and while a blanket is not the same as a warm, breathing body, it still provides heat and something with which to snuggle. You will want to wash your pup's bedding frequently in case he has an accident in his crate, and replace or remove any blanket that becomes ragged and starts to fall apart.

Your local pet shop should have a wide assortment of kennels and crates. Select one that is strong, durable and large enough to comfortably house your Basset when he is fully grown.

you have the money and the inclination to buy a new crate every time your pup has a growth spurt, it is better to get one that will accommodate your dog both as a pup and at full size. A medium or large sized crate will be necessary for a full-grown Basset, as the approximate weight range of a male Basset is between 55 and 75 pounds, with the bitch weighing approximately 10 pounds less.

CRATE TRAINING TIP
Puppies are naturally clean animals and will not soil their crate unless they have been left there too long. Also, the crate should not be overly large as the puppy will think it's okay to soil one end of the crate if he can get away from the 'accident' and sleep at the other end.

Toys

Toys are a must for dogs of all ages, especially for curious playful pups. Puppies are the 'children' of the dog world, and what child does not love toys? Chew toys provide enjoyment to both dog and owner—your dog will enjoy playing with his favourite toys, while you will enjoy the fact that they distract him from your expensive shoes and leather sofa. Puppies love to chew; in fact, chewing is a physical need for pups as they are teething, and everything looks appetising! The full range of your possessions—from old tea towel to Oriental carpet—are fair game in the eyes of a teething pup. Puppies are not all that discerning when it comes to finding something to literally 'sink their teeth into'—everything tastes great!

Basset puppies are fairly aggressive chewers and only the hardest, strongest toys should be offered to them. Breeders advise owners to resist stuffed toys, because they can become de-stuffed in no time. The overly excited pup may ingest the stuffing, which is neither digestible nor nutritious.

Similarly, squeaky toys are quite popular, but must be avoided for the Basset. Perhaps a squeaky toy can be used as an aid in training, but not for free play. If a pup 'disembowels' one

CRATE TRAINING TIPS

During crate training, you should partition off the section of the crate in which the pup stays. If he is given too big an area, this will hinder your training efforts. Crate training is based on the fact that a dog does not like to soil his sleeping quarters, so it is ineffective to keep a pup in a crate that is so big that he can eliminate in one end and get far enough away from it to sleep. Also, you want to make the crate den-like for the pup. Blankets and a favourite toy will make the crate cosy for the small pup; as he grows, you may want to evict some of his 'roommates' to make more room.

It will take some coaxing at first, but be patient. Given some time to get used to it, your pup will adapt to his new home-within-a-home quite nicely.

TOYS, TOYS, TOYS!

With a big variety of dog toys available, and so many that look like they would be a lot of fun for a dog, be careful in your selection. It is amazing what a set of puppy teeth can do to an innocent-looking toy, so, obviously, safety is a major consideration. Be sure to choose the most durable products that you can find. Hard nylon bones and toys are a safe bet, and many of them are offered in different scents and flavours that will be sure to capture your dog's attention. It is always fun to play a game of catch with your dog, and there are balls and flying discs that are specially made to withstand dog teeth.

of these, the small plastic squeaker inside can be dangerous if swallowed. Monitor the condition of all your pup's toys carefully and get rid of any that have been chewed to the point of becoming potentially dangerous.

Be careful of natural bones, which have a tendency to splinter into sharp, dangerous pieces. Also be careful of rawhide, which can turn into pieces that are easy to swallow or into a mushy mess on your carpet. Best are the multi-flavoured bones made of materials meant for hours of chewing and which do not break off into dangerous small pieces. These come in a variety of

Purchase toys specifically designed for dogs. Most pet shops offer a vast array.

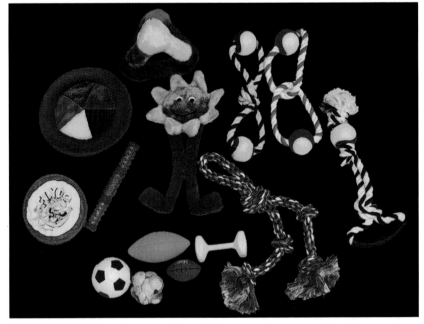

flavours that appeal to dogs: liver, chicken, bacon, etc.

LEAD
A nylon lead is probably the best option as it is the most resistant to puppy teeth should your pup take a liking to chewing on his lead. Of course, this is a habit that should be nipped in the bud, but if your pup likes to chew on his lead he has a very slim chance of being able to chew through the strong nylon. Nylon leads are also lightweight, which is good for a young Basset who is just getting used to the idea of walking on a lead. For everyday walking and safety purposes, the nylon lead is a good choice. As your pup grows

MENTAL AND DENTAL
Toys not only help your puppy get the physical and mental stimulation he needs but also provide a great way to keep his teeth clean. Hard rubber or nylon toys, especially those constructed with grooves, are designed to scrape away plaque, preventing bad breath and gum infection.

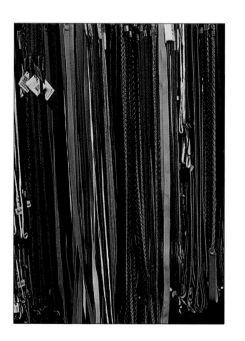

up and gets used to walking on the lead, you may want to purchase a flexible lead. These leads allow you to extend the length to give the dog a broader area to explore or to shorten the length to keep the dog close to you. Of course, there are special leads for training purposes, but these are not necessary for routine walks.

COLLAR
Your pup should get used to wearing a collar all the time since you will want to attach his ID tags to it. You have to attach the lead to something! A lightweight nylon collar is a

Your local pet shop will have a wide assortment of leads from which you can choose the one which best suits your needs.

When purchasing food and water bowls for your Basset Hounds, consider those pendulous ears in your selection. Enquire about special bowls for Bassets that are designed to keep the dogs' ears out of their bowl.

good choice; make sure that it fits snugly enough so that the pup cannot wriggle out of it, but is loose enough so that it will not be uncomfortably tight around the pup's neck. You should be able to fit a finger between the pup and the collar. It may take some time for your pup to get used to wearing the collar, but soon he will not even notice that it is there. Choke collars are made for training, but should only be used by an experienced handler.

FOOD AND WATER BOWLS

Your pup will need at least two bowls, one for food and one for water. You may want two sets of bowls, one for inside and one for outside, depending on where the dog will be fed and where he will be spending most of his time. Stainless steel or sturdy plastic bowls are popular choices. Plastic bowls are more chewable. Dogs tend not to chew on the steel variety, which can be sterilised. It is important to buy sturdy bowls since anything is in danger of being chewed by puppy teeth and you do not want your dog to be constantly chewing apart his bowl (for his safety and for your purse!).

CLEANING SUPPLIES

Until a pup is housetrained you will be doing a lot of cleaning. Accidents will occur, which is

Choose the Proper Collar

The BUCKLE COLLAR is the standard collar used for everyday purpose. Be sure that you adjust the buckle on growing puppies. Check it every day. It can become too tight overnight! These collars can be made of leather or nylon. Attach your dog's identification tags to this collar.

The CHOKE COLLAR is the usual collar recommended for training. It is constructed of highly polished steel so that it slides easily through the stainless steel loop. The idea is that the dog controls the pressure around its neck and he will stop pulling if the collar becomes uncomfortable. Never leave a choke collar on your dog when not training.

The HALTER is for a trained dog that has to be restrained to prevent running away, chasing a cat and the like. Considered the most humane of all collars, it is frequently used on dogs for which collars are not comfortable.

NATURAL TOXINS

Examine your grass and garden landscaping before bringing your puppy home. Many varieties of plants have leaves, stems or flowers that are toxic if ingested, and you can depend on a curious puppy to investigate them. Ask your vet for information on poisonous plants or research them at your library.

okay in the beginning because the puppy does not know any better. All you can do is be prepared to clean up any 'accidents.' Old rags, towels, newspapers and a safe disinfectant are good to have on hand.

BEYOND THE BASICS

The items previously discussed are the bare necessities. You will find out what else you need as you go along—grooming supplies, flea/tick protection, baby gates to partition a room, etc. These things will vary depending on your situation but it is important that you have

everything you need to feed and make your Basset comfortable in his first few days at home.

PUPPY-PROOFING YOUR HOME

Aside from making sure that your Basset will be comfortable in your home, you also have to make sure that your home is safe for your Basset. This means taking precautions that your pup will not get into anything he should not get into and that there is nothing within his reach that may harm him should he sniff it, chew it, inspect it, etc. This probably seems obvious since,

PUPPY-PROOFING

Thoroughly puppy-proof your house before bringing your puppy home. Never use roach or rodent poisons in any area accessible to the puppy. Avoid the use of toilet cleaners. Most dogs are born with 'toilet sonar' and will take a drink if the lid is left open. Also keep the rubbish secured and out of reach.

while you are primarily concerned with your pup's safety, at the same time you do not want your belongings to be ruined. Breakables should be placed out of reach if your dog is to have full run of the house. If he is to be limited to certain places within the house, keep any

CHEMICAL TOXINS

Scour your garage for potential puppy dangers. Remove weed killers, pesticides and antifreeze materials. Antifreeze is highly toxic and even a few drops can kill an adult dog. The sweet taste attracts the animal, who will quickly consume it from the floor or curbside.

Keep a close eye on your pup when he is outdoors. Many gardens are treated with herbicides and insecticides, which can harm your Basset if he walks on the grass or sniffs the flower beds.

potentially dangerous items in the 'off-limits' areas. An electrical cord can pose a danger should the puppy decide to taste it—and who is going to convince a pup that it would not make a great chew toy? Cords should be fastened tightly against the wall. If your dog is going to spend time in a crate, make sure that there is nothing near his crate that he can reach if he sticks his curious little nose or paws through the openings. Just as you would with a child, keep all household cleaners and chemicals where the pup cannot

get to them.

It is also important to make sure that the outside of your home is safe. Of course your

TOXIC PLANTS

Many plants can be toxic to dogs. If you see your dog carrying a piece of vegetation in his mouth, approach him in a quiet, disinterested manner, avoid eye contact, pet him and gradually remove the plant from his mouth. Alternatively, offer him a treat and maybe he'll drop the plant on his own accord. Be sure no toxic plants are growing in your own garden.

puppy should never be unsupervised, but a pup let loose in the garden will want to run and explore, and he should be granted that freedom. Do not let a fence give you a false sense of security; you would be surprised how crafty (and persistent) a dog can be in working out how to dig under and squeeze his way through small holes, or to climb over a fence. The remedy is to make the fence high enough so that it really is impossible for your dog to get over it (about 2 metres should suffice), and well embedded into the ground. Be sure to repair or secure any gaps in the fence. Check the fence periodically to ensure that it is in good shape and make repairs as needed; a very determined pup may return to the same spot to 'work on it' until he is able to get through.

TRAVEL TIP
Taking your dog from the breeder to your home in a car can be a very uncomfortable experience for both of you. The puppy will have been taken from his warm, friendly, safe environment and brought into a strange new environment. An environment that moves! Be prepared for loose bowels, urination, crying, whining and even fear biting. With proper love and encouragement when you arrive home, the stress of the trip should quickly disappear.

GIVE HIM LOTS OF LOVE
It will take at least two weeks for your puppy to become accustomed to his new surroundings. Give him lots of love, attention, handling, frequent opportunities to relieve himself, a diet he likes to eat and a place he can call his own.

FIRST TRIP TO THE VET
You have picked out your puppy, and your home and family are ready. Now all you have to do is collect your Basset from the breeder and the fun begins, right? Well…not so fast. Something else you need to prepare is your pup's first trip to the veterinary surgeon. Perhaps the breeder can recommend someone in the area who specialises in Bassets, or maybe you know some other Basset

owners who can suggest a good vet. Either way, you should have an appointment arranged for your pup before you pick him up and plan on taking him for an examination before bringing him home.

The pup's first visit will consist of an overall examination to make sure that the pup does not have any problems that are not apparent to the eye. The veterinary surgeon will also set up a schedule for the pup's vaccinations; the breeder will inform you of which ones the pup has already received and the vet can continue from there.

INTRODUCTION TO THE FAMILY

Everyone in the house will be excited about the puppy coming home and will want to pet him and play with him, but it is best to make the introduction low-key so as not to overwhelm the puppy. He is apprehensive already. It is the first time he has been separated from his mother and the breeder, and the ride to your home is likely the first time he has been in a car. The last thing you want to do is smother him, as this will only frighten him further. This is not to say that human contact is not extremely necessary at this stage, because this is the time when a connection between the pup and his human family is formed.

HOW VACCINES WORK

If you've just bought a puppy, you surely know the importance of having your pup vaccinated, but do you understand how vaccines work? Vaccines contain the same bacteria or viruses that cause the disease you want to prevent, but they have been chemically modified so that they don't cause any harm. Instead, the vaccine causes your dog to produce antibodies that fight the harmful bacteria. Thus, if your pup is exposed to the disease in the future, the antibodies will destroy the viruses or bacteria.

Gentle petting and soothing words should help console him, as well as just putting him down and letting him explore on his own (under your watchful eye, of course).

The pup may approach the family members or may busy

FEEDING TIP

You will probably start feeding your pup the same food that he has been getting from the breeder; the breeder should give you a few days' supply to start you off. Although you should not give your pup too many treats, you will want to have puppy treats on hand for coaxing, training, rewards, etc. Be careful, though, as a small pup's calorie requirements are relatively low and a few treats can add up to almost a full day's worth of calories without the required nutrition.

new people, new noises, new smells, and new things to investigate: so be gentle, be affectionate, and be as comforting as you can be.

PUPPY'S FIRST NIGHT HOME
You have travelled home with your new charge safely in his crate or a friend's lap. He's been to the vet for a thorough check-up; he's been weighed, his papers examined; perhaps he's even been vaccinated and wormed as well. He's met the family, licked the whole family, including the excited children and the less-than-happy cat. He's explored his area, his new bed, the garden and anywhere else he's been permitted. He's eaten his first meal at home and relieved himself in the proper place. He's heard lots of new sounds, smelled new friends and seen more of the outside world than ever before.

That was just the first day! He's worn out and is ready for bed...or so you think!

It's puppy's first night and you are ready to say 'Good night'—keep in mind that this is puppy's first night ever to be sleeping alone. His dam and littermates are no longer at paw's length and he's a bit scared, cold and lonely. Be reassuring to your new family member. This is not the time to spoil him and give in to his inevitable whining.

himself with exploring for a while. Gradually, each person should spend some time with the pup, one at a time, crouching down to get as close to the pup's level as possible and letting him sniff their hands and petting him gently. He definitely needs human attention and he needs to be touched—this is how to form an immediate bond. Just remember that the pup is experiencing a lot of things for the first time, at the same time. There are

Puppies whine. They whine to let the others know where they are and hopefully to get company out of it. Place your pup in his new bed or crate in his room and close the door. Mercifully, he may fall asleep without a peep. When the inevitable occurs, ignore the whining: he is fine. Be strong and keep his interests in mind. Do not allow your heart to become guilty and visit the pup. He will fall asleep.

Many breeders recommend placing a piece of bedding from his former home in his new bed so that he recognises the scent of his littermates. Others like to fill an old sock with other old socks making a puppy-like lump for the puppy to snuggle with. Others still advise placing a hot water bottle in his bed for warmth. This latter may be a good idea provided the pup does

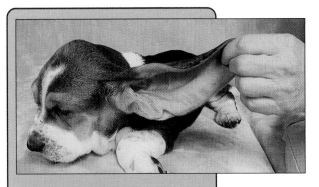

REGULAR EAR CLEANING IS A MUST

The Basset's long pendulous ears are susceptible to otitis externa or what your family might simply call 'smelly ears'! Cleaning your Basset's ear canals as regularly as you clip his toenails is a good preventative measure. Ask your veterinary surgeon for an ear wash or you can make your own by mixing together in equal amounts, isopropyl alcohol and white vinegar.

PUPPY PROBLEMS

The majority of problems that are commonly seen in young pups will disappear as your dog gets older. However, how you deal with problems when he is young will determine how he reacts to discipline as an adult dog. It is important to establish who is boss (hopefully it will be you!) right away when you are first bonding with your dog. This bond will set the tone for the rest of your life together.

not attempt to suckle—he will get good and wet and may not fall asleep so fast.

Puppy's first night can be somewhat stressful for the pup and his new family. Remember that you are setting the tone of nighttime at your house. Unless you want to play with your pup every evening at 10 p.m., midnight and 2 a.m., don't initiate the habit. Your family will thank you, and so will your pup!

SOCIALISATION

Thorough socialisation includes not only meeting new people but also being introduced to new experiences such as riding in the car, having his coat brushed, hearing the television, walking in a crowd—the list is endless. The more your pup experiences, and the more positive the experiences are, the less of a shock and the less frightening it will be for your pup to encounter new things.

PREVENTING PUPPY PROBLEMS

SOCIALISATION

Now that you have done all of the preparatory work and have helped your pup get accustomed to his new home and family, it is about time for you to have some fun! Socialising your Basset pup gives you the opportunity to show off your new friend, and your pup gets to reap the benefits of being an adorable furry creature that people will want to pet and, in general, think is absolutely precious!

Besides getting to know his new family, your puppy should be exposed to other people, animals and situations, but of course he must not come into close contact with dogs you don't know well until his course of injections is fully complete. This will help him become well adjusted as he grows up and less prone to being timid or fearful of the new things he will encounter. Your pup's socialisation began at the breeder's but now it is your responsibility to continue it. The socialisation he receives up until the age of 12 weeks is the most critical, as this is the time when he forms his impressions of the outside world. Be especially careful during the eight-to-ten-week period, also known as the fear period. The interaction he receives during this time should be gentle and reassuring. Lack of socialisation can manifest itself in fear and aggression as the dog grows up. He needs lots of human contact, affection, handling and exposure to other animals.

Once your pup has received his necessary vaccinations, feel free to take him out and about (on his lead, of course). Walk him around the neighbourhood, take him on your daily errands, let people pet him, let him meet other dogs and pets, etc. Puppies do not have to try to make friends; there will be no shortage of people who will want to introduce themselves. Just make sure that you carefully supervise each meeting. If the neighbourhood children want to say hello, for example, that is great—children and pups most often make great companions. Sometimes an excited child can unintentionally handle a pup too roughly, or an overzealous pup can playfully nip a little too hard. You want to make socialisation experiences positive ones. What a pup learns during this very formative stage will affect his attitude toward future encounters. You want your dog to be comfortable around everyone. A pup that has a bad experience with a child may grow up to be a dog that is shy around or aggressive toward children.

CONSISTENCY IN TRAINING

Dogs, being pack animals, naturally need a leader, or else they try to establish dominance in their packs. When you bring a dog into your family, the choice of who becomes the leader and who becomes the 'pack' is entirely up to you! Your pup's intuitive quest for dominance, coupled with the fact that it is nearly impossible to look at an

adorable Basset pup, with his 'puppy-dog' eyes, his soft forlorn expression, his floppy ears, and not cave in, give the pup almost an unfair advantage in getting the upper hand! A pup will

MANNERS MATTER

During the socialisation process, a puppy should meet people, experience different environments and definitely be exposed to other canines. Through playing and interacting with other dogs, your puppy will learn lessons, ranging from controlling the pressure of his jaws by biting his litter mates to the inner-workings of the canine pack that he will apply to his human relationships for the rest of his life. That is why removing a puppy from its litter too early (before eight weeks) can be detrimental to the pup's development.

definitely test the waters to see what he can and cannot do. Do not give in to those soulful eyes—stand your ground when it comes to disciplining the pup and make sure that all family members do the same. It will only confuse the pup when Mother tells him to get off the sofa when he is used to sitting up there with Father to watch the nightly news. Avoid discrepancies by having all members of the household decide on the rules before the pup even comes home…and be consistent in enforcing them! Early training shapes the dog's personality, so you cannot be unclear in what you expect.

COMMON PUPPY PROBLEMS

The best way to prevent puppy problems is to be proactive in stopping an undesirable behaviour as soon as it starts. The old saying 'You can't teach an old dog new tricks' does not necessarily hold true, but it is true that it is much easier to discourage bad behaviour in a young developing pup than to wait until the pup's bad behaviour becomes the adult dog's bad habit. There are some problems that are especially prevalent in puppies as they develop.

NIPPING

As puppies start to teethe, they feel the need to sink their teeth into anything available…unfortunately that includes your fingers, arms, hair, and toes. You may find this behaviour cute for the first five seconds…until you feel just how sharp those puppy teeth are. This is something you want to discourage immediately and consistently with a firm 'No!' (or whatever number of firm 'No's' it takes for him to understand that you mean business). Then replace your finger with an appropriate chew toy. While this behaviour is merely annoying when the dog is young, it can become dangerous as your Basset's adult teeth grow in and his jaws develop, and he continues to think it is okay to gnaw on human appendages. Your Basset does not mean any harm with a friendly nip, but he also does not know his own strength.

CRYING/WHINING

Your pup will often cry, whine, whimper, howl or make some type of commotion when he is left alone. This is basically his way of calling out for attention to make sure that you know he is there and that you have not forgotten about him. He feels insecure when he is left alone, when you are out of the house and he is in his crate or when you are in another part of the house and he cannot see you. The noise he is making is an expression of the anxiety he feels at being alone, so he needs to be taught that being alone is okay. You are not actually training the dog to stop making noise, you are training him to feel comfortable when he is alone and thus removing the need for him to make the noise. This is where the crate filled with cosy bedding and toys comes in handy. You want to know that he is safe when you are not there to supervise, and you know that he will be safe in his crate rather than roaming freely about the house. In order for the pup to stay in his crate without making a fuss, he needs to be comfortable in his crate. On that note, it is extremely important that the crate is never used as a form of punishment, or the pup will have a negative association with the crate.

Accustom the pup to the crate in short, gradually increasing time intervals in which you put him in the crate, maybe with a treat, and stay in the room with him. If he cries or makes a fuss, do not go to him, but stay in his sight. Gradually he will realise that staying in his crate is all right without your help, and it will not be so traumatic for him when you are not around. You may want to leave the radio on softly when you leave the house; the sound of human voices may be comforting to him.

CHEWING TIPS
Chewing goes hand in hand with nipping in the sense that a teething puppy is always looking for a way to soothe his aching gums. In this case, instead of chewing on you, he may have taken a liking to your favourite shoe or something else which he should not be chewing. Again, realise that this is a normal canine behaviour that does not need to be discouraged, only redirected. Your pup just needs to be taught what is acceptable to chew on and what is off limits. Consistently tell him NO when you catch him chewing on something forbidden and give him a chew toy. Conversely, praise him when you catch him chewing on something appropriate. In this way you are discouraging the inappropriate behaviour and reinforcing the desired behaviour. The puppy chewing should stop after his adult teeth have come in, but an adult dog continues to chew for various reasons—perhaps because he is bored, perhaps to relieve tension or perhaps he just likes to chew. That is why it is important to redirect his chewing when he is still young.

DIETARY AND FEEDING CONSIDERATIONS

Today the choices of food for your Basset Hound are many and varied. There are simply dozens of brands of food in all sorts of flavours and textures, ranging from puppy diets to those for seniors. There are even hypoallergenic and low-calorie diets available. Because your Basset's food has a bearing on coat, health and temperament, it is essential that the most suitable diet be selected for a Basset of his age. It is fair to say, however, that even dedicated owners can be somewhat perplexed by the enormous range of foods available. Only understanding what is best for your dog will help you reach a valued decision.

> ### FEEDING TIP
> You must store your dried dog food carefully. Open packages of dog food quickly lose their vitamin value, usually within 90 days of being opened. Mould spores and vermin could also contaminate the food.

> ### TEST FOR PROPER DIET
> A good test for proper diet is the colour, odour and firmness of your dog's stool. A healthy dog usually produces three semi-hard stools per day. The stools should have no unpleasant odour. They should be the same colour from excretion to excretion.

Dog foods are produced in three basic types: dried, semi-moist and tinned. Dried foods are useful for the cost-conscious for overall they tend to be less expensive than semi-moist or tinned. These contain the least fat and the most preservatives. In general tinned foods are made up of 60–70 percent water, while semi-moist ones often contain so much sugar that they are perhaps the least preferred by owners, even though their dogs seem to like them.

When selecting your dog's diet, three stages of development must be considered: the puppy stage, adult stage and the senior or veteran stage.

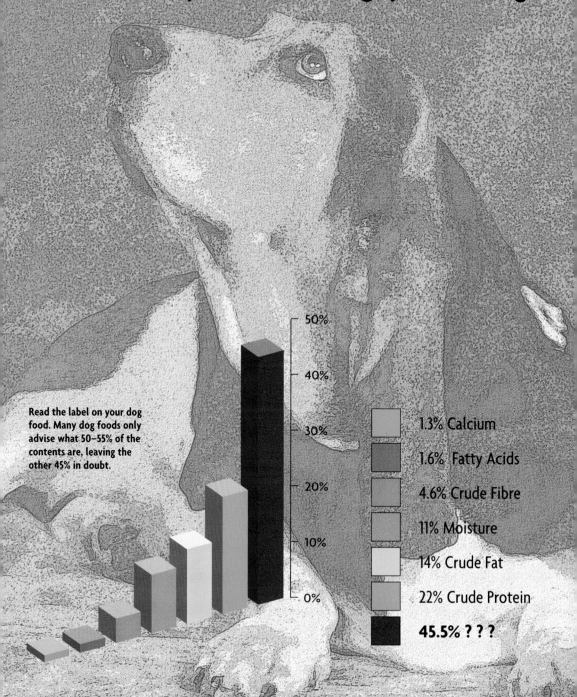

What are you feeding your dog?

Read the label on your dog food. Many dog foods only advise what 50–55% of the contents are, leaving the other 45% in doubt.

1.3% Calcium

1.6% Fatty Acids

4.6% Crude Fibre

11% Moisture

14% Crude Fat

22% Crude Protein

45.5% ? ? ?

FEEDING TRIALS MATTER MOST

There are many varieties of dried food available for your Basset. There are arguments among veterinary scientists as to the value of nutrient analyses (protein, fat, fibre, moisture, ash, cholesterol, minerals, etc.). All agree that feeding trials are what matters, but you also have to consider the individual Basset Hound's activity and age. It is likely that your Basset's breeder has long ago decided which dried food works best for his or her line of Bassets and it is best to stick with the breeder's recommendations. Remember, as he ages, the senior citizen Basset will require a food that is lower in protein and fat. However, at any age, if the dog develops digestive, skin or weight problems a consultation with your veterinary surgeon is probably a good idea to discover the cause and discuss your Basset's current dietary needs.

PUPPY STAGE

Puppies instinctively want to suck milk from their mother's teats and a normal puppy will exhibit this behaviour from just a few moments following birth. If puppies do not attempt to suckle within the first half-hour or so, they should be encouraged to do so by placing them on the nipples, having selected ones with plenty of milk. This early milk supply is important in providing colostrum to protect the puppies during the first eight to ten weeks of their lives. Although a mother's milk is much better than any milk formula, despite there being some excellent ones available, if the puppies do not feed you will have to feed them yourself. For those with less experience, advice from a veterinary surgeon is important so that you feed not only the right quantity of milk but that of correct quality, fed at suitably frequent intervals, usually every two hours during the first few days of life.

Puppies should be allowed to nurse from their mothers for about the first six weeks, although from the third or fourth week you will have begun to introduce small portions of suitable solid food. Most breeders like to introduce alternate milk and meat meals initially, building up to weaning time.

By the time the puppies are seven or a maximum of eight weeks old, they should be fully weaned and fed solely on a proprietary puppy food. Selection of the most suitable, good-quality diet at this time is essential for a puppy's fastest growth rate is during the first year of life. Veterinary surgeons are usually able to offer advice in this regard and, although the frequency of meals will have been reduced over time, only when a puppy has reached the age of about 12 months should an adult diet be fed.

Puppy and junior diets should be well balanced for the needs of your dog, so that except in certain circumstances additional vitamins, minerals and proteins will not be required.

ADULT DIETS

A dog is considered an adult when it has stopped growing, so in general the diet of a Basset can be changed to an adult one at about 10 to 12 months of age. Again you should rely upon your veterinary surgeon or dietary specialist to recommend an acceptable maintenance diet. Major dog food manufacturers specialise in this type of food, and it is just necessary for you to select the one best suited to your dog's needs. Active dogs may have different requirements than sedate dogs.

SENIOR DIETS

As dogs get older, their metabolism changes. The older dog

FEEDING TIPS

Dog food must be at room temperature, neither too hot nor too cold. Fresh water, changed daily and served in a clean bowl, is mandatory, especially when feeding dried food.

Never feed your dog from the table while you are eating. Never feed your dog leftovers from your own meal. They usually contain too much fat and too much seasoning.

Dogs must chew their food. Hard pellets are excellent; soups and slurries are to be avoided.

Don't add left-overs or any extras to normal dog food. The normal food is usually balanced and adding something extra destroys the balance.

Except for age-related changes, dogs do not require dietary variations. They can be fed the same diet, day after day, without their becoming ill.

DO DOGS HAVE TASTE BUDS?

Watching a dog 'wolf' or gobble his food, seemingly without chewing, leads an owner to wonder whether their dogs can taste anything. Yes, dogs have taste buds, with sensory perception of sweet, salty and sour. Puppies are born with fully mature taste buds.

DRINK, DRANK, DRUNK— MAKE IT A DOUBLE

In both humans and dogs, as well as most living organisms, water forms the major part of nearly every body tissue. Naturally, we take water for granted, but without it, life as we know it would cease.

For dogs, water is needed to keep their bodies functioning biochemically. Additionally, water is needed to replace the water lost while panting. Unlike humans who are able to sweat to dissipate heat, dogs must pant to cool down, thereby losing the vital water from their bodies needed to regulate their body temperatures. Humans lose electrolyte-containing products and other body-fluid components through sweating; dogs do not lose anything except water.

Water is essential always, but especially so when the weather is hot or humid or when your dog is exercising or working vigorously.

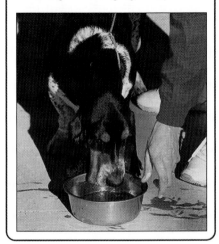

usually exercises less, moves more slowly and sleeps more. This change in lifestyle and physiological performance requires a change in diet. Since these changes take place slowly, they might not be recognisable. What is easily recognisable is weight gain. By continuing to feed your dog an adult-maintenance diet when it is slowing down metabolically, your dog will gain weight. Obesity in an older dog compounds the health problems that already accompany old age.

As your dog gets older, few of his organs function up to par. The kidneys slow down and the intestines become less efficient. These age-related factors are best handled with a change in diet and a change in feeding schedule to give smaller portions that are more easily digested.

There is no single best diet for every older dog. While many dogs do well on light or senior diets, other dogs do better on puppy diets or other special premium diets such as lamb and rice. Be sensitive to your senior Basset's diet and this will help control other problems that may arise with your old friend.

WATER

Just as your dog needs proper nutrition from his food, water is an essential 'nutrient' as well. Water keeps the dog's body properly hydrated and promotes normal function of the body's systems. Your Basset should have a bowl of water available to him inside your home, as well as outdoors. Make sure that the dog's water bowls are clean, and change the water often. Small water bowls are made especially to attach to the crate door and are recommended when your Basset is left in his crate for three or four hours at a time, or overnight. During housebreaking it is necessary to keep an eye on how much water your Basset is drinking, but once he is reliably trained he should have access to clean fresh water at all times, especially if you feed dried food.

TIPPING THE SCALES

Good nutrition is vital to your dog's health, but many people end up over-feeding or giving unnecessary supplements. Here are some common doggie diet don'ts:

- Adding milk, yoghurt and cheese to your dog's diet may seem like a good idea for coat and skin care, but dairy products are very fattening and can cause indigestion.
- Diets high in fat will not cause heart attacks in dogs but will certainly cause your dog to gain weight.
- Most importantly, don't assume your dog will simply stop eating once he doesn't need any more food. Given the chance, he will eat you out of house and home!

'DOES THIS COLLAR MAKE ME LOOK FAT?'

While humans may obsess about how they look and how trim their bodies are, many people believe that extra weight on their dogs is a good thing. The truth is, pets should not be over- or under-weight, as both can lead to or signal sickness. In order to tell how fit your pet is, run your hands over his ribs. Are his ribs buried under a layer of fat or are they sticking out consider-ably? If your pet is within his normal weight range, you should be able to feel the ribs easily. If you stand above him, the outline of his body should resemble an hourglass. Some breeds do tend to be leaner; while some are a bit stockier, but making sure your dog is the right weight for his breed will certainly contribute to his good health.

EXERCISE

Although a Basset has short legs, all dogs require some form of exercise, regardless of breed. A sedentary lifestyle is as harmful to a dog as it is to a person. Regular walks, play sessions in the garden, or letting the dog run free in the garden under your supervi-sion are all sufficient forms of exercise for the Basset. Remember until your Basset is fully mature exercise must be kept in modera-tion. The Basset puppy needs time to grow up and develop stamina before you embark on more strenuous forms of exercise such as overly long walks. Remember to rule out any forms of jumping when playing with your Basset.

Bear in mind that an

Feed your Basset Hound a sensible, balanced diet. Do not overindulge your Basset. Remember a Basset Hound is always starving unless he's eating!

overweight dog should never be suddenly over-exercised; instead he should be allowed to increase exercise slowly. Just as when beginning an exercise programme for yourself, introduce your Basset to exercise slowly and build up gradually. The slim, trim, well-muscled adult Basset will be able to keep up with you on long walks but do not include him on a morning run. While he will run on his own for a bit, those short legs and that heavy body preclude him from becoming a distance runner. You will notice that the Basset does not look like a Whippet! Not only is exercise essential to keep the dog's body fit, it is essential to his mental well-being. A bored dog will find something to do, which often manifests itself in some type of destructive behaviour. In this sense, it is essential for the owner's mental well-being as well!

GROOMING

BRUSHING
A natural bristle brush, a slicker brush or a hound glove can be used for regular routine brushing. Daily brushing is effective for removing dead hair and stimulating the dog's natural oils to add shine and a healthy look to the coat. Although the Basset's coat is short and close, it does require a five-minute once-over to

WALKING LIKE A PRO
For many people it is difficult to imagine putting your dog's well being in someone else's hands, but if you are unable to give your dog his necessary exercise breaks, hiring a professional dog walker may be a good idea. Dog walkers offer your dog exercise, a chance to work off energy and companionship—all things that keep your dog healthy. Seek referrals from your veterinary surgeon, breeder or groomer to find a reputable dog walker.

keep it looking its shiny best. Regular grooming sessions are also a good way to spend time with your dog. Many dogs grow to like the feel of being brushed and will enjoy the daily routine.

Basset Hounds do not require extensive grooming. Your local pet shop will have all the tools necessary to keep your dog looking neat and tidy.

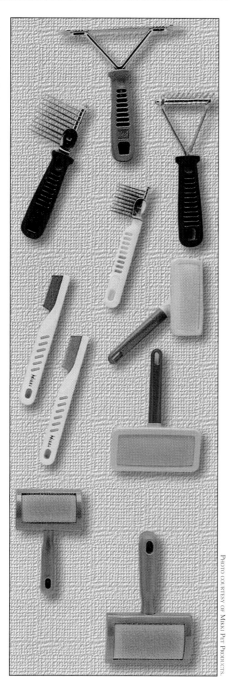

PHOTO COURTESY OF MIKKI PET PRODUCTS.

BATHING

Dogs do not need to be bathed as often as humans, but regular bathing is essential for healthy skin and a healthy, shiny coat. With the Basset, bathing is recommended regularly—perhaps every two weeks—to minimise any doggy odour to which this loose-skinned, long-eared breed is prone. Again, like most anything, if you accustom your pup to being bathed as a puppy, it will be second nature by the time he grows up. You want your dog to be at ease in the bath or else it could end up a wet, soapy, messy ordeal for both of you!

Brush your Basset thoroughly before wetting his coat. This will get rid of any dust or tangles.

GROOMING EQUIPMENT

How much grooming equipment you purchase will depend on how much grooming you are going to do. Here are some basics:

- Natural bristle brush
- Hound glove
- Slicker brush
- Metal comb
- Scissors
- Blaster
- Rubber mat
- Dog shampoo
- Spray hose attachment
- Ear cleaner
- Cotton wipes
- Towels
- Nail clippers

Make sure that your dog has a good non-slip surface to stand on. Begin by wetting the dog's coat. A shower or hose attachment is necessary for thoroughly wetting and rinsing the coat. Check the water temperature to make sure that it is neither too hot nor too cold.

Next, apply shampoo to the dog's coat and work it into a good lather. You should purchase a shampoo all the way down to the skin. You can use this opportunity to check the skin for any bumps, bites or other abnormalities. Do not neglect any area of the body— get all of the hard-to-reach places, including the groin and underbelly.

Once the dog has been thoroughly shampooed, he requires an equally thorough rinsing. Shampoo left in the coat

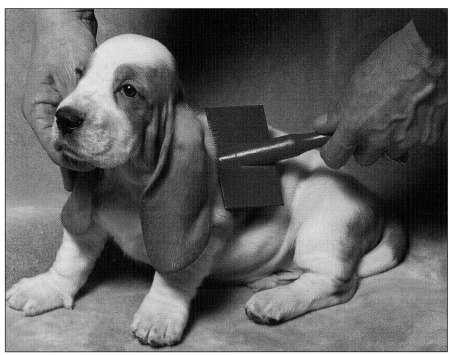

You should brush your Basset for about five minutes every day. Start when the Basset is a puppy so he will become accustomed to the brushing procedure.

shampoo that is made for dogs. Do not use a product made for human hair. Wash the head last; you do not want shampoo to drip into the dog's eyes while you are washing the rest of his body. Work the can be irritating to the skin. Protect his eyes from the shampoo by shielding them with your hand and directing the flow of water in the opposite direction. You should also avoid getting water in the ear

Clean around the Basset's eyes with a piece of soft cotton to avoid tear stains or residue.

Bassets have extraordinarily long ears. The ears require regular cleaning and examination for parasites.

canal. Be prepared for your dog to shake out his coat—you might want to stand back, but make sure you have a hold on the dog to keep him from running through the house.

EAR CLEANING

Ears are an area of concern for most Basset owners. Do not neglect the ears during your weekly once-over brushing. The ears should be kept clean and any excess hair inside the ear should be carefully cut. Ears can be cleaned with a cotton wipe and special cleaner or ear powder made especially for dogs. Be on the lookout for any signs of infection or ear mite infestation. If your Basset has been shaking his head or

scratching at his ears frequently, this usually indicates a problem. If his ears have an unusual odour, this is a sure sign of mite infestation or infection, and a signal to have his ears checked by the veterinary surgeon.

NAIL CLIPPING

Your Basset should be accustomed to having his nails trimmed at an early age, since it will be part of your maintenance routine throughout his life. Not only does it look nicer, but long nails can scratch someone unintentionally. Also, a long nail has a better chance of ripping and bleeding, or causing the feet to spread. A

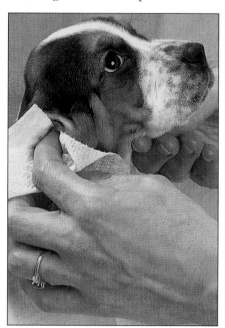

good rule of thumb is that if you can hear your dog's nails clicking on the floor when he walks, his nails are too long.

Before you start cutting, make sure you can identify the 'quick' in each nail. The quick is a blood vessel that runs through the centre of each nail and grows rather close to the end. It will bleed if accidentally cut, which will be quite painful for the dog as it contains nerve endings. Keep some type of clotting agent on hand, such as a styptic pencil or styptic powder (the type used for shaving). This will stop the bleeding quickly when applied to the end of the cut nail. Do not panic if you cut the quick, just stop the bleeding and talk soothingly to your dog. Once he has calmed down, move on to the next nail. It is better to clip a little at a time, particularly with black-nailed dogs.

Hold your pup steady as you begin trimming his nails; you do not want him to make any sudden movements or run away. Talk to him soothingly and stroke him as you clip. Holding his foot in your hand, simply take off the end of each nail in one quick clip. You can purchase nail clippers that are specially made for dogs; you can probably find them wherever you buy pet or grooming supplies.

Nail Maintenance

Nail Casing

Quick

Cut Line

Dark-Coloured Nails

With black or dark nails, where the quick is not easy to see, it's best to clip only the tip of the nail or to use a file.

Light-Coloured Nails

In light-coloured nails, clipping is much simpler because you can see the vein (or quick) that grows inside the casing.

Your dog's nails should be trimmed regularly. When you can hear the nails clicking as the dog walks on a hard surface, the nails are too long. Pet shops sell special clippers for dog's nails.

DID YOU KNOW?

A dog that spends a lot of time outside on a hard surface, such as cement or pavement, will have his nails naturally worn down and may not need to have them trimmed as often, except maybe in the colder months when he is not outside as much. Regardless, it is best to get your dog accustomed to this procedure at an early age so that he is used to it. Some dogs are especially sensitive about having their feet touched, but if a dog has experienced it since he was young, he should not be bothered by it.

TRAVELLING WITH YOUR DOG

CAR TRAVEL

You should accustom your Basset to riding in a car at an early age. You may or may not take him in the car often, but at the very least he will need to go to the vet and you do not want these trips to be traumatic for the dog or problematic for you. The safest way for a dog to ride in the car is in his crate. If he uses a crate in the house, you can use the same crate for travel, if your vehicle can accommodate it. Put the pup in the crate and see how he reacts. If the puppy seems uneasy, you can have a passenger hold him on his lap while you drive but you will need to find another solution by the time your dog is fully grown. Another option is a specially made safety harness for dogs, which straps the dog in much like a seat belt. Do not let the dog roam loose in the vehicle—this is very dangerous! If you should stop short, your dog can be thrown and injured. If the dog starts climbing on you and pestering you while you are driving, you will not be able to concentrate on the road. It is an unsafe situation for everyone—human and canine.

For long trips, be prepared to stop to let the dog relieve himself. Bring along whatever you need to clean up after him. You should take along some paper kitchen towels and perhaps some old towelling for use should he have an accident in the car or suffer from travel sickness.

AIR TRAVEL

While it is possible to take a dog on a flight within Britain, this is fairly unusual and advance permission is always required. The dog will be required to travel in a fibreglass crate and you should always check in advance with the airline regarding specific requirements. To help the dog be at ease, put one of his favourite toys in the crate with him. Do not feed the dog for at least six hours before the trip to minimise his need to relieve himself. However, certain regulations specify that water must always be made available to the dog in the crate.

Make sure your dog is properly identified and that your contact information appears on his ID tags and on his crate. Animals travel in a different area of the plane than human passengers so every rule must be strictly followed so as to prevent the risk of getting separated from your dog.

BOARDING

So you want to take a family holiday—and you want to include all members of the family. You would probably make arrangements for accommodations ahead of time anyway, but this is especially important when travelling with a dog. You do not want to make an overnight stop at the

Select a suitable boarding kennel close to your home. Visit the facility before you actually need to engage their services.

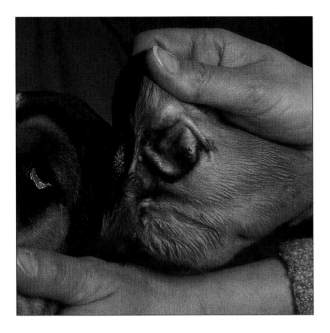

clean they are and where the dogs are kept. Talk to some of the employees and see how they treat the dogs—do they spend time with the dogs, play with them, exercise them, etc.? Also find out the kennel's policy on vaccinations and what they require. This is for all of the dogs' safety, since when dogs are kept together, there is a greater risk of diseases being passed from dog to dog.

IDENTIFICATION

Your Basset is your valued companion and friend. That is why you always keep a close eye on him and you have made sure that he cannot escape from the garden or wriggle out of his collar and run away from you. However, accidents can happen and there

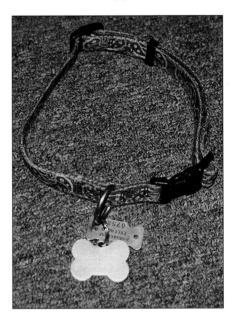

Given the size of the Basset's ears, some owners opt to tattoo the dog in this location.

Identification tags are an absolute necessity for every dog. Your local pet shop or veterinary surgeon can assist you in obtaining proper tags.

only place around for miles and find out that they do not allow dogs. Also, you do not want to reserve a place for your family without confirming that you are travelling with a dog because if it is against their policy you may not have a place to stay.

Alternatively, if you are travelling and choose not to bring your Basset, you will have to make arrangements for him while you are away. Some options are to take him to a neighbour's house to stay while you are gone, to have a trusted neighbour stop by often or stay at your house, or bring your dog to a reputable boarding kennel. If you choose to board him at a kennel, you should visit in advance to see the facility, how

IDENTIFICATION OPTIONS

As puppies become more and more expensive, especially those puppies of high quality for showing and/or breeding, they have a greater chance of being stolen. The usual collar dog tag is, of course, easily removed. But there are two techniques that have become widely used for identification.

The puppy microchip implantation involves the injection of a small microchip, about the size of a corn kernel, under the skin of the dog. If your dog shows up at a clinic or shelter, or is offered for resale under less than savoury circumstances, it can be positively identified by the microchip. The microchip is scanned and a registry quickly identifies you as the owner. This is not only protection against theft, but should the dog run away or go chasing a squirrel and get lost, you have a fair chance of getting it back.

Tattooing is done on various parts of the dog, from its belly to its cheeks. The number tattooed can be your telephone number or any other number which you can easily memorise. When professional dog thieves see a tattooed dog, they usually lose interest in it. Both microchipping and tattooing can be done at your local veterinary clinic. For the safety of our dogs, no laboratory facility or dog broker will accept a tattooed dog as stock.

may come a time when your dog unexpectedly gets separated from you. If this unfortunate event should occur, the first thing on your mind will be finding him.

Proper identification, including an ID tag, a tattoo, and possibly a microchip, will increase the chances of his being returned to you safely and quickly.

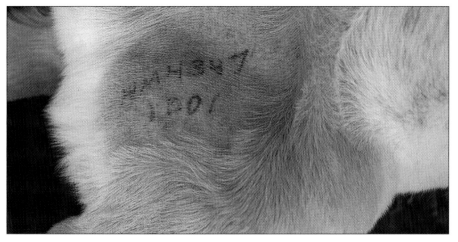

The belly is the preferred place to tattoo any dog, as shown on this Basset Hound.

Housebreaking and Training Your
BASSET HOUND

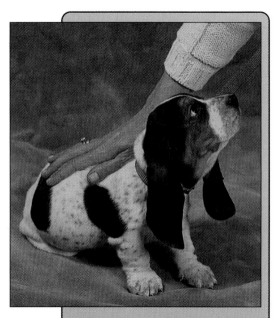

BUILDING A LASTING RELATIONSHIP

If you start with a normal, healthy dog and give him time, patience and some carefully executed lessons, you will reap the rewards of that training for the life of the dog. And what a life it will be! The two of you will find immeasurable pleasure in the companionship you have built together with love, respect and understanding.

Living with an untrained dog is much like owning a piano that you do not know how to play—it is a nice object to look at but it does not do much more than that to bring you pleasure. Now try taking piano lessons and suddenly the piano comes alive and brings forth magical sounds and rhythms that set your heart singing and your body swaying.

The same is true with your Basset Hound. Any dog is a big responsibility and if not trained sensibly may develop unacceptable behaviour that annoys you or could even cause family friction.

To train your Basset, you may like to enrol in an obedience class. Teach him good manners as you learn how and why he behaves the way he does. Find out how to communicate with your dog and how to recognise and understand his communications with you. Suddenly the dog takes on a new role in your life—he is smart, interesting, well behaved and fun to be with. He demonstrates his bond of devotion to you daily. In other words, your Basset does wonders for your ego because he constantly reminds you that you are not only his leader, you are his hero!

Those involved with teaching dog obedience and counselling owners about their dogs' behaviour have discovered some interesting facts about dog ownership. For example, training dogs when they are puppies results in the highest rate of success in developing well-mannered and well-adjusted adult dogs. Training an older dog, from six months to six years of age, can produce almost equal results providing that the owner accepts the dog's slower rate of learning capability and is willing to work patiently to help the dog succeed at developing to his fullest potential. Unfortunately, many owners of untrained adult dogs lack the patience factor, so they do not persist until their dogs are successful at learning particular behaviours.

Training a puppy aged 10 to 16 weeks (20 weeks at the most) is like working with a dry sponge in a pool of water. The pup soaks up whatever you show him and constantly looks for more things to do and learn. At this early age, his body is not yet producing hormones, and therein lies the reason for such a high rate of success. Without hormones, he is focused on his owners and not particularly interested in investigating other places, dogs, people,

BETTER PARENTING
Training a dog is a life experience. Many parents admit that much of what they know about raising children they learned from caring for their dogs. Dogs respond to love, fairness and guidance, just as children do. Become a good dog owner and you may become an even better parent.

etc. You are his leader: his provider of food, water, shelter and security. He latches onto you and wants to stay close. He will usually follow you from room to room, will not let you out of his sight when you are outdoors with him, and will respond in like manner to the people and animals you encounter. If you greet a friend warmly, he will be happy to greet the person as well. If, however, you are hesitant, even anxious, about the approach of a

YOUR HANDS WILL DO THE TALKING

To a dog's way of thinking, your hands are like his mouth in terms of a defence mechanism. If you squeeze him too tightly, he might just bite you because that would be his normal response. This is not aggressive biting and, although all biting should be discouraged, you need the discipline in learning how to handle your dog.

stances, the solution to the problem of lack of lesson availability lies within the pages of this book.

This chapter is devoted to helping you train your Basset Hound at home. If the recommended procedures are followed faithfully, you may expect positive results that will prove rewarding to both you and your dog.

Whether your new charge is a puppy or a mature adult, the methods of teaching and the techniques we use in training basic behaviours are the same. After all, no dog, whether puppy or adult, likes harsh or inhumane methods. All creatures, however, respond favourably to gentle motivational methods and sincere praise and encouragement. Now let us get started.

HOUSEBREAKING

You can train a puppy to relieve itself wherever you choose, but this must be somewhere suitable.

stranger, he will respond accordingly.

Once the puppy begins to produce hormones, his natural curiosity emerges and he begins to investigate the world around him. It is at this time when you may notice that the untrained dog begins to wander away from you and even ignore your commands to stay close.

There are usually classes within a reasonable distance of the owner's home, but you also do a lot to train your dog yourself. Sometimes there are classes available but the tuition is too costly. Whatever the circum-

Your local pet shop will have devices that are designed to assist you in cleaning up after your dog.

You should bear in mind from the outset that when your puppy is old enough to go out in public places, any canine deposits must be removed at once. You will always have to carry with you a small plastic bag or 'poop-scoop.'

Outdoor training includes such surfaces as grass, dirt and cement. Indoor training usually means training your dog to newspaper.

When deciding on the surface and location that you will want your Basset to use, be sure it is going to be permanent. Training your dog to grass and then changing your mind two months later is extremely difficult for both dog and owner.

Next, choose the command you will use each and every time you want your puppy to void. 'Go hurry up' and 'Toilet' are examples of commands commonly used by dog owners.

Get in the habit of giving the puppy your chosen relief command before you take him out. That way, when he becomes an adult, you will be able to determine if he wants to go out when you ask him. A confirmation will be signs of interest, wagging his tail, watching you intently, going to the door, etc.

PUPPY'S NEEDS

Puppy needs to relieve himself after play periods, after each meal, after he has been sleeping and any time he indicates that he is looking for a place to urinate or defecate.

The urinary and intestinal tract muscles of very young puppies are not fully developed. Therefore, like human babies, puppies need to relieve themselves frequently.

Take your puppy out often—every hour for an eight-week-old, for example, and always immedi-

CONSISTENCY PAYS OFF

Dogs need consistency in their feeding schedule, exercise and toilet breaks and in the verbal commands you use. If you use 'Stay' on Monday and 'Stay here, please' on Tuesday, you will confuse your dog. Don't demand perfect behaviour during training classes and then let him have the run of the house the rest of the day. Above all, lavish praise on your pet consistently every time he does something right. The more he feels he is pleasing you, the more willing he will be to learn.

A LITTLE ATTENTION

Dogs will do anything for your attention. If you reward the dog when he is calm and resting, you will develop a well-mannered dog. If, on the other hand, you greet your dog excitedly and encourage him to wrestle with you, the dog will greet you the same way and you will have a hyperactive dog on your hands.

ately after sleeping and eating. The older the puppy, the less often he will need to relieve himself. Finally, as a mature healthy adult, he will require only three to five relief trips per day.

HOUSING

Since the types of housing and control you provide for your puppy has a direct relationship on the success of housetraining, we consider the various aspects of both before we begin training.

Bringing a new puppy home and turning him loose in your house can be compared to turning a child loose in a sports arena and telling the child that the place is all his! The sheer enormity of the place would be too much for him to handle.

Instead, offer the puppy clearly defined areas where he can play, sleep, eat and live. A room of the house where the family gathers is the most obvious choice. Puppies are social animals and need to feel a part of the pack right from the start. Hearing your voice, watching you while you are doing things and smelling you nearby are all positive reinforcers that he is now a member of your pack. Usually a sitting room, the kitchen or a nearby adjoining breakfast area is ideal for providing safety and security for both puppy and owner.

Within that room there should be a smaller area which the puppy can call his own. An alcove, a wire or fibreglass dog crate or a fenced (not boarded!) corner from which he can view the activities of his new family will be fine. The size of the area or crate is the key factor here. The area must be large enough for the puppy to lie down and stretch out as well as stand up without rubbing his head on the top, yet small enough so that he cannot relieve himself at one end and sleep at the other

CANINE DEVELOPMENT SCHEDULE

It is important to understand how and at what age a puppy develops into adulthood. If you are a puppy owner, consult the following Canine Development Schedule to determine the stage of development your puppy is currently experiencing. This knowledge will help you as you work with the puppy in the weeks and months ahead.

Period	Age	Characteristics
FIRST TO THIRD	**BIRTH TO SEVEN WEEKS**	Puppy needs food, sleep and warmth, and responds to simple and gentle touching. Needs mother for security and disciplining. Needs littermates for learning and interacting with other dogs. Pup learns to function within a pack and learns pack order of dominance. Begin socialising with adults and children for short periods. Begins to become aware of its environment.
FOURTH	**EIGHT TO TWELVE WEEKS**	Brain is fully developed. Needs socialising with outside world. Remove from mother and littermates. Needs to change from canine pack to human pack. Human dominance necessary. Fear period occurs between 8 and 16 weeks. Avoid fright and pain.
FIFTH	**THIRTEEN TO SIXTEEN WEEKS**	Training and formal obedience should begin. Less association with other dogs, more with people, places, situations. Period will pass easily if you remember this is pup's change-to-adolescence time. Be firm and fair. Flight instinct prominent. Permissiveness and over-disciplining can do permanent damage. Praise for good behaviour.
JUVENILE	**FOUR TO EIGHT MONTHS**	Another fear period about 7 to 8 months of age. It passes quickly, but be cautious of fright and pain. Sexual maturity reached. Dominant traits established. Dog should understand sit, down, come and stay by now.

without coming into contact with his droppings until fully trained to relieve himself outside.

Dogs are, by nature, clean animals and will not remain close to their relief areas unless forced to do so. In those cases, they then become dirty dogs and usually remain that way for life.

The designated area should be lined with clean bedding and

THE MOST HONOURABLE ANIMAL

Dogs are the most honourable animals in existence. They consider another species (humans) as their own. They interface with you. You are their leader. Puppies perceive children to be on their level; their actions around small children are different from their behaviour around their adult masters.

For Basset Hounds that live in the city without easy access to the outdoors, newspaper training is the housebreaking method of choice.

a toy. Water must always be available, in a non-spill container.

CONTROL

By control, we mean helping the puppy to create a lifestyle pattern that will be compatible to that of his human pack (YOU!). Just as we guide little children to learn our way of life, we must show the puppy when it is time to play, eat, sleep, exercise and even entertain himself.

Your puppy should always sleep in his crate. He should also learn that, during times of household confusion and excessive human activity such as at breakfast when family members are preparing for the day, he can play by himself in relative safety and comfort in his designated area. Each time you leave the puppy alone, he should understand exactly where he is to stay. You can gradually increase the time he is left alone to get him used to it.

Puppies are chewers. They cannot tell the difference between lamp cords, television wires, shoes, table legs, etc. Chewing into a television wire, for example, can be fatal to the puppy while a shorted wire can start a fire in the house. If the puppy chews on the arm of the chair when he is alone, you will probably discipline him angrily when you get home. Thus, he makes the association that your coming home means he is going to be punished. (He will not remember chewing up the chair and is incapable of making the association of the discipline with his naughty deed.)

Other times of excitement, such as family parties, etc., can be fun for the puppy providing he can view the activities from the security of his designated area. He is not underfoot and he is not being fed all sorts of titbits that will probably cause him stomach distress, yet he still feels a part of the fun.

SCHEDULE

A puppy should be taken to his relief area each time he is released from his designated area, after meals, after a play session, when he first awakens in the morning (at age eight weeks, this can mean 5 a.m.!). The puppy will indicate that he's ready 'to go' by circling or sniffing busily—do not

MEALTIME

Mealtime should be a peaceful time for your puppy. Do not put his food and water bowls in a high-traffic area in the house. For example, give him his own little corner of the kitchen where he can eat undisturbed and where he will not be underfoot. Do not allow small children or other family members to disturb the pup when he is eating.

THE STUDENT'S STRESS TEST

During training sessions you must be able to recognise signs of stress in your dog such as:
• tucking his tail between his legs
• lowering his head
• shivering or trembling
• standing completely still or running away
• panting and/or salivating
• avoiding eye contact
• flattening his ears back
• urinating submissively
• rolling over and lifting a leg
• grinning or baring teeth
• aggression when restrained

If your four-legged student displays these signs he may just be nervous or intimidated. The training session may have been too lengthy with not enough praise and affirmation. Stop for the day and try again tomorrow.

misinterpret these signs. For a puppy less than ten weeks of age, a routine of taking him out every hour is necessary. As the puppy grows, he will be able to wait for longer periods of time.

Keep trips to his relief area short. Stay no more than five or six minutes and then return to the house. If he goes during that time, praise him lavishly and take him indoors immediately. If he does not, but he has an accident when you go back indoors, pick him up immediately, say 'No! No!' and return to his relief area. Wait a few minutes, then return to the house again. Never hit a puppy or rub his face in urine or excrement when he has an accident!

Once indoors, put the puppy in his crate until you have had time to clean up his accident. Then release him to the family area and watch him more closely than before. Chances are, his accident was a result of your not picking up his signal or waiting too long before offering him the opportunity to relieve himself. Never hold a grudge against the puppy for accidents.

Let the puppy learn that going outdoors means it is time to relieve himself, not play. Once trained, he will be able to play indoors and out and still differentiate between the times for play versus the times for relief.

Help him develop regular hours for naps, being alone,

THE GOLDEN RULE

The golden rule of dog training is simple. For each 'question' (command), there is only one correct answer (reaction). One command = one reaction. Keep practising the command until the dog reacts correctly without hesitating. Be repetitive but not monotonous. Dogs get bored just as people do!

PRACTICE MAKES PERFECT!

• Have training lessons with your dog every day in several short segments—three to five times a day for a few minutes at a time is ideal.
• Do not have long practice sessions. The dog will become easily bored.
• Never practise when you are tired, ill, worried or in an otherwise negative mood. This will transmit to the dog and may have an adverse effect on its performance.

Think fun, short and above all POSITIVE! End each session on a high note, rather than a failed exercise, and make sure to give a lot of praise. Enjoy the training and help your dog enjoy it, too.

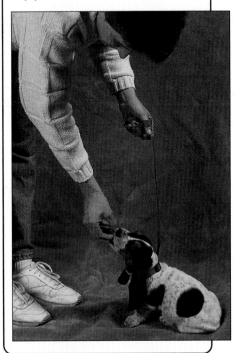

playing by himself and just resting, all in his crate. Encourage him to entertain himself while you are busy with your activities. Let him learn that having you near is comforting, but it is not your main purpose in life to provide him with undivided attention.

Each time you put a puppy in his own area, use the same command, whatever suits best. Soon, he will run to his crate or special area when he hears you say those words.

Crate training provides safety for you, the puppy and the home. It also provides the puppy with a feeling of security, and that helps the puppy achieve self-confidence and clean habits.

Remember that one of the primary ingredients in housetraining your puppy is control. Regardless of your lifestyle, there will always be occasions when you will need to have a place where your dog can

HOW MANY TIMES A DAY?

AGE	RELIEF TRIPS
To 14 weeks	10
14–22 weeks	8
22–32 weeks	6
Adulthood	4
(dog stops growing)	

These are estimates, of course, but they are a guide to the MINIMUM opportunities a dog should have each day to relieve itself.

ROLES OF DISCIPLINE, REWARD AND PUNISHMENT

Discipline, training one to act in accordance with rules, brings order to life. It is as simple as that. Without discipline, particularly in a group society, chaos reigns supreme and the group will eventually perish. Humans and canines are social animals and need some form of discipline in order to function effectively. They must procure food, protect their home base and their young and reproduce to keep the species going.

If there were no discipline in the lives of social animals, they would eventually die from starvation and/or predation by other stronger animals.

In the case of domestic canines, dogs need discipline in their lives in order to understand how their pack (you and other family members) functions and how they must act in order to survive.

stay and be happy and safe. Crate training is the answer for now and in the future.

In conclusion, a few key elements are really all you need for a successful housetraining method—consistency, frequency, praise, control and supervision. By following these procedures with a normal, healthy puppy, you and the puppy will soon be past the stage of 'accidents' and ready to move on to a full and rewarding life together.

THINK BEFORE YOU BARK

Dogs are sensitive to their master's moods and emotions. Use your voice wisely when communicating with your dog. Never raise your voice at your dog unless you are angry and trying to correct him. 'Barking' at your dog can become as meaningless as 'dogspeak' is to you. Think before you bark!

A large humane society in a highly populated area recently surveyed dog owners regarding their satisfaction with their relationships with their dogs. People who had trained their dogs were 75% more satisfied with their pets than those who had never trained their dogs.

Dr Edward Thorndike, a psychologist, established *Thorndike's Theory of Learning*, which states that a behaviour that results in a pleasant event tends to be repeated. A behaviour that results in an unpleasant event tends not to be repeated. It is this theory on which training methods are based today. For example, if you manipulate a dog to perform a specific behaviour and reward him for doing it, he is likely to do it again because he enjoyed the end result.

Occasionally, punishment, a penalty inflicted for an offence, is necessary. The best type of punishment often comes from an outside source. For example, a child is told not to touch the

THE SUCCESS METHOD

1 Tell the puppy 'Crate time!' and place him in the crate with a small treat (a piece of cheese or half of a biscuit). Let him stay in the crate for five minutes while you are in the same room. Then release him and praise lavishly. Never release him when he is fussing. Wait until he is quiet before you let him out.

2 Repeat Step 1 several times a day.

3 The next day, place the puppy in the crate as before. Let him stay there for ten minutes. Do this several times.

4 Continue building time in five-minute increments until the puppy stays in his crate for 30 minutes with you in the room. Always take him to his relief area after prolonged periods in his crate.

5 Now go back to Step 1 and let the puppy stay in his crate for five minutes, this time while you are out of the room.

6 Once again, build crate time in five-minute increments with you out of the room. When the puppy will stay willingly in his crate (he may even fall asleep!) for 30 minutes with you out of the room, he will be ready to stay in it for several hours at a time.

6 Steps to Successful Crate Training

chasing the cat but the cat turns and swipes a claw across the dog's face, leaving him with a painful gash on his nose. The final result is that the dog stops chasing the cat.

TRAINING EQUIPMENT

COLLAR AND LEAD

For a Basset the collar and lead that you use for training must be one with which you are easily able to work, not too heavy for the dog and perfectly safe.

TREATS

Have a bag of treats on hand. Something nutritious and easy to swallow works best. Use a soft treat, a chunk of cheese or a piece of cooked chicken rather than a dry biscuit. By the time the dog gets done chewing a dry treat, he will forget why he is being rewarded in the first place! Using food rewards will

stove because he may get burned. He disobeys and touches the stove. In doing so, he receives a burn. From that time on, he respects the heat of the stove and avoids contact with it. Therefore, a behaviour that results in an unpleasant event tends not to be repeated.

A good example of a dog learning the hard way is the dog who chases the house cat. He is told many times to leave the cat alone, yet he persists in teasing the cat. Then, one day he begins not teach a dog to beg at the table—the only way to teach a dog to beg at the table is to give him food from the table. In training, rewarding the dog with a food treat will help him associate praise and the treats with learning new behaviours that obviously please his owner.

TRAINING BEGINS: ASK THE DOG A QUESTION

In order to teach your dog anything, you must first get his attention. After all, he cannot learn anything if he is looking away from you with his mind on something else.

To get his attention, ask him, 'School?' and immediately walk over to him and give him a treat as you tell him 'Good dog.' Wait a minute or two and repeat the routine, this time with a treat in your hand as you approach within a foot of the dog. Do not go directly to him, but stop about a foot short of him and hold out the treat as you ask, 'School?' He will see you approaching with a treat in your hand and most likely begin walking toward you. As you meet, give him the treat and praise again.

The third time, ask the question, have a treat in your hand and walk only a short distance toward the dog so that he must walk almost all the way to you. As he reaches you, give

For a young Basset Hound, a lightweight nylon collar is suitable to accustom the puppy to the idea of wearing a collar.

him the treat and praise again.

By this time, the dog will probably be getting the idea that if he pays attention to you, especially when you ask that question, it will pay off in treats and enjoyable activities for him. In other words, he learns that 'school' means doing things with you that result in treats and positive attention for him.

Remember that the dog does not understand your verbal language, he only recognises sounds. Your question translates to a series of sounds for him, and those sounds become the signal to go to you and pay attention; if he does, he will get to interact with you plus receive treats and praise.

HOUSEBREAKING TIP

Never line your pup's sleeping area with newspaper. Puppy litters are usually raised on newspaper and, once in your home, the puppy will immediately associate newspaper with voiding. Never put newspaper on any floor while housetraining, as this will only confuse the puppy. If you are paper-training him, use paper in his designated relief area ONLY. Finally, restrict water intake after evening meals. Offer a few licks at a time—never let a young puppy gulp water after meals.

THE BASIC COMMANDS

TEACHING SIT

Now that you have the dog's attention, attach his lead and hold it in your left hand and a food treat in your right. Place your food hand at the dog's nose and let him lick the treat but not take it from you. Say 'Sit' and slowly raise your food hand from in front of the dog's nose up over his head so that he

TRY, TRY AGAIN

Dogs are as different from each other as people are. What works for one dog may not work for another. Have an open mind. If one method of training is unsuccessful, try another.

is looking at the ceiling. As he bends his head upward, he will have to bend his knees to maintain his balance. As he bends his knees, he will assume a sit position. At that point, release the food treat and praise lavishly with comments such as 'Good dog! Good sit!', etc. Remember to always praise enthusiastically, because dogs relish verbal praise from their owners and feel so proud of themselves whenever they accomplish a behaviour.

You will not use food forever in getting the dog to obey your commands. Food is only used to teach new behaviours, and once the dog knows what you want when you give a specific command, you will wean him off the food treats but still maintain the verbal praise. After all, you will always have your voice with you, and there will be many times when you have no food rewards but expect the dog to obey.

TEACHING DOWN

Teaching the down exercise is easy when you understand how the dog perceives the down position, and it is very difficult when you do not. Dogs perceive the down position as a submissive one, therefore teaching the down exercise using a forceful method can sometimes make the dog develop such a fear of the down that he either runs away when you say 'Down' or he attempts to snap at the person who tries to force him down.

Have the dog sit close alongside your left leg, facing in the same direction as you are. Hold the lead in your left hand and a food treat in your right. Now place your left hand lightly on the top of the dog's shoulders where they meet above the spinal cord. Do not push down on the dog's shoulders; simply rest your left hand there so you can guide the

TRAINING TIP
Stand up straight and authoritatively when giving your dog commands. Do not issue commands when lying on the floor or lying on your back on the sofa. If you are on your hands and knees when you give a command, your dog will think you are positioning yourself to play.

dog to lie down close to your left leg rather than to swing away from your side when he drops.

Now place the food hand at the dog's nose, say 'Down' very softly (almost a whisper), and slowly lower the food hand to the dog's front feet. When the food hand reaches the floor, begin moving it forward along

> **TRAINING TIP**
>
> Your dog is actually training you at the same time you are training him. Dogs do things to get attention. They usually repeat whatever succeeds in getting your attention.

the floor in front of the dog. Keep talking softly to the dog, saying things like, 'Do you want this treat? You can do this, good dog.' Your reassuring tone of voice will help calm the dog as he tries to follow the food hand in order to get the treat.

When the dog's elbows touch the floor, release the food and praise softly. Try to get the dog to maintain that down position for several seconds before you let him sit up again. The goal here is to get the dog to settle down and not feel threatened in the down position.

TEACHING STAY

It is easy to teach the dog to stay in either a sit or a down position. Again, we use food and praise during the teaching process as we help the dog to understand exactly what it is that we are expecting him to do.

To teach the sit/stay, start with the dog sitting on your left side as before and hold the lead in your left hand. Have a food treat in your right hand and

> **TRAINING TIP**
>
> A dog in jeopardy never lies down. He stays alert on his feet because instinct tells him that he may have to run away or fight for his survival. Therefore, if a dog feels threatened or anxious, he will not lie down. Consequently, it is important to have the dog calm and relaxed as he learns the down exercise.

place your food hand at the dog's nose. Say 'Stay' and step out on your right foot to stand directly in front of the dog, toe to toe, as he licks and nibbles the treat. Be sure to keep his head facing upward to maintain the sit position. Count to five and then swing around to stand next to the dog again with him on your left. As soon as you get back to the original position, release the food and praise lavishly.

To teach the down/stay, do the down as previously described. As soon as the dog lies down, say 'Stay' and step out on your right foot just as you did in the sit/stay. Count to five and then return to stand beside the dog with him on your left side. Release the treat and praise as always.

Within a week or ten days, you can begin to add a bit of distance between you and your dog when you leave him. When you do, use your left hand open with the palm facing the dog as a stay signal, much the same as the hand signal a constable uses to stop traffic at an intersection. Hold the food treat in your right hand as before, but this time the food is not touching the dog's nose. He will watch the food hand and quickly learn that he is going to get that treat as soon as you return to his side.

When you can stand 1 metre

HELPING PAWS

Your dog may not be the next Lassie, but every pet has the potential to do some tricks well. Identify his natural talents and hone them. Is your dog always happy and upbeat? Teach him to wag his tail or give you his paw on command. Real homebodies can be trained to do household chores, such as carrying dirty washing or retrieving the morning paper.

away from your dog for 30 seconds, you can then begin building time and distance in both stays. Eventually, the dog

can be expected to remain in the stay position for prolonged periods of time until you return to him or call him to you. Always praise lavishly when he stays.

TEACHING COME

If you make teaching 'come' a rewarding experience, you should never have a 'student' that does not love the game or that fails to come when called. The secret, it seems, is never to teach the word 'come.'

At times when an owner most wants his dog to come when called, the owner is likely upset or anxious and he allows these feelings to come through in the tone of his voice when he calls his dog. Hearing that desperation in his owner's voice, the dog fears the results of going to him and therefore either disobeys outright or runs in the opposite direction. The secret, therefore, is to teach the dog a game and, when you want him to come to you, simply play the game. It is practically a no-fail solution!

To begin, have several members of your family take a few food treats and each go into a different room in the house. Take turns calling the dog, and each person should celebrate the dog's finding him with a treat and lots of happy praise. When a person calls the dog, he

TRAINING TIP

When calling the dog, do not say 'Come.' Say things like, 'Rover, where are you? See if you can find me! I have a biscuit for you!' Keep up a constant line of chatter with coaxing sounds and frequent questions such as, 'Where are you?' The dog will learn to follow the sound of your voice to locate you and receive his reward.

FEAR AGGRESSION

Pups who are subjected to physical abuse during training commonly end up with behavioural problems as adults. One common result of abuse is fear aggression, in which a dog will lash out, bare his teeth, snarl and finally bite someone by whom he feels threatened. For example, your daughter may be playing with the dog one afternoon. As they play hide-and-seek, she backs the dog into a corner, and as she attempts to tease him playfully, he bites her hand. Examine the cause of this behaviour. Did your daughter ever hit the dog? Did someone who resembles your daughter hit or scream at the dog? Fortunately, fear aggression is relatively easy to correct. Have your daughter engage in only positive activities with the dog, such as feeding, petting and walking. She should not give any corrections or negative feedback. If the dog still growls or cowers away from her, allow someone else to accompany them. After approximately one week, the dog should feel that he can rely on her for many positive things, and he will also be prevented from reacting fearfully towards anyone who might resemble her.

is actually inviting the dog to find him and get a treat as a reward for 'winning.'

A few turns of the 'Where are you?' game and the dog will work out that everyone is playing the game and that each person has a big celebration awaiting his success at locating them. Once he learns to love the game, simply calling out 'Where are you?' will bring him running from wherever he is when he hears that all-important question.

The come command is recognised as one of the most important things to teach a dog, but there are trainers who work with thousands of dogs and never teach the actual word 'Come.' Yet these dogs will race to respond to a person who uses the dog's name followed by 'Where are you?' For example, a woman has a 12-year-old companion dog who went blind, but who never fails to locate her owner when asked, 'Where are you?'

Children particularly love to play this game with their dogs. Children can hide in smaller places like a shower or bath, behind a bed or under a table. The dog needs to work a little bit harder to find these hiding places, but when he does he loves to celebrate with a treat and a tussle with a favourite youngster.

TEACHING HEEL

Heeling means that the dog walks beside the owner without pulling. It takes time and patience on the owner's part to succeed at teaching the dog that he (the owner) will not proceed unless the dog is walking calmly beside him. Pulling out ahead on the lead is definitely not acceptable.

Begin with holding the lead in your left hand as the dog sits beside your left leg. Move the loop end of the lead to your right hand but keep your left hand short on the lead so it

SAFETY FIRST

While it may seem that the most important things to your dog are eating, sleeping and chewing the upholstery on your furniture, his first concern is actually safety. The domesticated dogs we keep as companions have the same pack instinct as their ancestors who ran free thousands of years ago. Because of this pack instinct, your dog wants to know that he and his pack are not in danger of being harmed, and that his pack has a strong, capable leader. You must establish yourself as the leader early on in your relationship. That way your dog will trust that you will take care of him and the pack, and he will accept your commands without question.

TRAINING TIP

Teach your dog to HEEL in an enclosed area. Once you think the dog will obey reliably and you want to attempt advanced obedience exercises such as off-lead heeling, test him in a fenced-in area so he cannot run away.

keeps the dog in close next to you.

Say 'Heel' and step forward on your left foot. Keep the dog close to you and take three steps. Stop and have the dog sit next to you in what we now call the 'heel position.' Praise verbally, but do not touch the dog. Hesitate a moment and begin again with 'Heel,' taking three steps and stopping, at which point the dog is told to sit again.

Your goal here is to have the dog walk those three steps

without pulling on the lead. When he will walk calmly beside you for three steps without pulling, increase the number of steps you take to five. When he will walk politely beside you while you take five steps, you can increase the length of your walk to ten steps. Keep increasing the length of your stroll until the dog will walk quietly beside you without pulling as long as you want him to heel. When you stop heeling, indicate to the dog that the exercise is over by verbally praising as you pet him and say 'OK, good dog.' The 'OK' is used as a release word meaning that the exercise is finished and the dog is free to relax.

If you are dealing with a dog who insists on pulling you around, simply 'put on your

TRAINING TIP

Dogs do not understand our language. They can be trained to react to a certain sound, at a certain volume. If you say 'No, Oliver' in a very soft pleasant voice it will not have the same meaning as 'No, Oliver!!' when you shout it as loud as you can. You should never use the dog's name during a reprimand, just the command NO!! Since dogs don't understand words, comics often use dogs trained with opposite meanings. Thus, when the comic commands his dog to SIT the dog will stand up, and vice versa.

TRAINING TIP

If you begin teaching the heel by taking long walks and letting the dog pull you along, he misinterprets this action as an acceptable form of taking a walk. When you pull back on the lead to counteract his pulling, he reads that tug as a signal to pull even harder!

brakes' and stand your ground until the dog realises that the two of you are not going anywhere until he is beside you and moving at your pace, not his. It may take some time just standing there to convince the dog that you are the leader and you will be the one to decide on

A well-trained Basset Hound is a pleasure to spend time with. Walking your Basset every day pays off in exercise and companionship for human and dog.

the direction and speed of your travel.

Each time the dog looks up at you or slows down to give a slack lead between the two of you, quietly praise him and say, 'Good heel. Good dog.' Eventually, the dog will begin to respond and within a few days he will be walking politely beside you without pulling on the lead. At first, the training

TRAINING TIP

Never call your dog to come to you for a correction or scold him when he reaches you. That is the quickest way to turn a 'Come' command into 'Go away fast!' Dogs think only in the present tense, and your dog will connect the scolding with coming to you, not with the misbehaviour of a few moments earlier.

sessions should be kept short and very positive; soon the dog will be able to walk nicely with you for increasingly longer distances. Remember also to give the dog free time and the opportunity to run and play when you have finished heel practice.

WEANING OFF FOOD IN TRAINING

Food is used in training new behaviours. Once the dog understands what behaviour goes with a specific command,

HOW TO WEAN THE 'TREAT HOG'

If you have trained your dog by rewarding him with a treat each time he performs a command, he may soon decide that without the treat, he won't sit, stay or come. The best way to fix this problem is to start asking your dog to do certain commands twice before being rewarded. Slowly increase the number of commands given and then vary the number: three sits and a treat one day, five sits for a biscuit the next day. Your dog will soon realise that there is no set number of sits before he gets his reward, and he'll likely do it the first time you ask in the hope of being rewarded sooner rather than later.

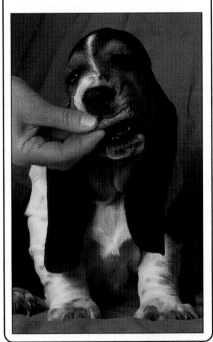

PLAY TIME

Play fetch games with your puppy in an enclosed area where he can retrieve his toy and bring it back to you. Always use a toy or object designated just for this purpose. Never use a shoe, stocking or other item he may later confuse with those in your wardrobe or underneath your chair.

BEGINNER'S CLASS

A basic obedience beginner's class usually lasts for six to eight weeks. Dog and owner attend an hour-long lesson once a week and practise for a few minutes, several times a day, each day at home. If done properly, the whole procedure will result in a well-mannered dog and an owner who delights in living with a pet that is eager to please and enjoys doing things with his owner.

it is time to start weaning him off the food treats. At first, give a treat after each exercise. Then, start to give a treat only after every other exercise. Mix up the times when you offer a food reward and the times when you only offer praise so that the dog will never know when he is going to receive both food and praise and when he is going to receive only praise. This is called a variable ratio reward system and it proves successful because there is always the chance that the owner will produce a treat, so the dog

never stops trying for that reward. No matter what, ALWAYS give verbal praise.

OBEDIENCE CLASSES

It is a good idea to enrol in an obedience class if one is available in your area. If yours is a show dog, ringcraft classes would be more appropriate. Many areas have dog clubs that offer basic obedience training as well as preparatory classes for obedience competition. There are also local dog trainers who offer similar classes.

At obedience trials, dogs can earn titles at various levels of competition. The beginning levels of competition include basic behaviours such as sit, down, heel, etc. The more advanced levels of competition include jumping, retrieving, scent discrimination and signal work. The advanced levels

OBEDIENCE SCHOOL

Taking your dog to an obedience school may be the best investment in time and money you can ever make. You will enjoy the benefits for the lifetime of your dog and you will have the opportunity to meet people with your similar expectations for companion dogs.

require a dog and owner to put a lot of time and effort into their training and the titles that can be earned at these levels of competition are very prestigious.

OTHER ACTIVITIES FOR LIFE

Whether a dog is trained in the structured environment of a class or alone with his owner at home, there are many activities that can bring fun and rewards to both owner and dog once they have mastered basic control.

Teaching the dog to help out around the home, in the garden or on the farm provides great satisfaction to both dog and owner. In addition, the dog's help makes life a little easier for his owner and raises his stature as a valued companion to his family. It helps give the dog a purpose by occupying his mind

> **DID YOU KNOW?**
> Occasionally, a dog and owner who have not attended formal classes have been able to earn entry-level titles by obtaining competition rules and regulations from a local kennel club and practising on their own to a degree of perfection. Obtaining the higher level titles, however, almost always requires extensive training under the tutelage of experienced instructors. In addition, the more difficult levels require more specialised equipment whereas the lower levels do not.

and providing an outlet for his energy.

If you are interested in participating in organised competition with your Basset, there are activities other than obedience in which you and your dog can become involved. Agility is a popular sport where dogs run through an obstacle course that includes various tunnels and other exercises to test the dog's speed and coordination. Bassets are not encouraged to undertake the various jumps that are part of some agility courses. The owners run through the course beside their dogs to give commands and to guide them through the course. Although competitive, the focus is on fun—it's fun to do, fun to watch, and great exercise.

> **EXERCISE**
> The puppy should also have regular play and exercise sessions when he is with you or a family member. Exercise for a very young puppy can consist of a short walk around the house or garden. Playing can include fetching games with a large ball or a special raggy. (All puppies teethe and need soft things upon which to chew.) Remember to restrict play periods to indoors within his living area (the family room, for example) until he is completely housetrained.

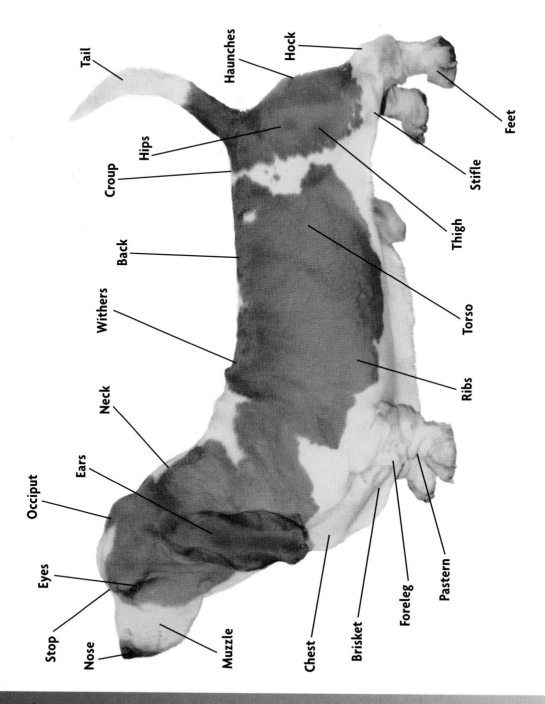

Physical Structure of the Basset Hound

Health Care for Your
BASSET HOUND

Dogs suffer many of the same physical illnesses as people. They might even share many of the same psychological problems. Since people usually know more about human diseases than canine maladies, many of the terms used in this chapter will be familiar but not necessarily those used by veterinary surgeons. We will use the term *x-ray*, instead of the more acceptable term *radiograph*. We will also use the familiar term *symptoms* even though dogs don't have symptoms, which are verbal descriptions of the patient's feelings: dogs have *clinical signs*. Since dogs can't speak, we have to look for clinical signs...but we still use the term *symptoms* in this book.

As a general rule, medicine is *practised*. That term is not arbitrary. Medicine is a constantly changing art as we learn more and more about genetics, electronic aids (like CAT scans) and daily laboratory advances. There are many dog maladies, like canine hip dysplasia, which are not universally treated in the same manner. Some veterinary surgeons

opt for surgery more often than others do.

SELECTING A VETERINARY SURGEON
Your selection of a veterinary surgeon should not be based upon personality (as most are) but upon their convenience to your home. You want a vet who is close because you might have emergencies or need to make multiple

Your chosen veterinary surgeon will become your Basset's best friend, next to you, of course. Do not make a hasty choice—choose your vet with care.

visits for treatments. You want a vet who has services that you might require such as microchipping and grooming facilities, as well as sophisticated pet supplies

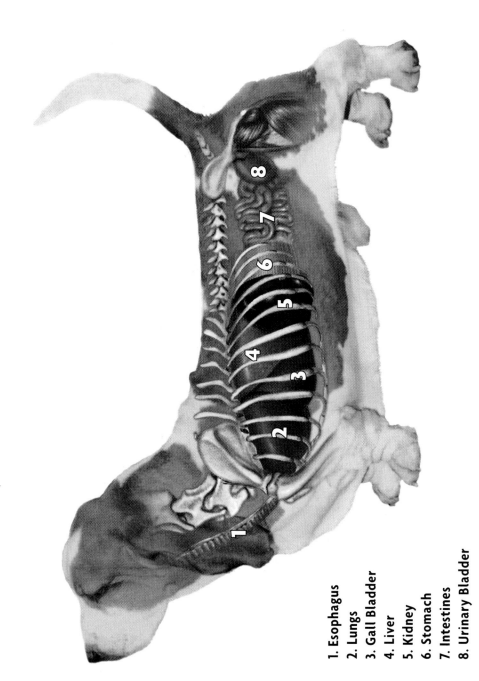

1. Esophagus
2. Lungs
3. Gall Bladder
4. Liver
5. Kidney
6. Stomach
7. Intestines
8. Urinary Bladder

Internal Organs of the Basset Hound

and a good reputation for ability and responsiveness. There is nothing more frustrating than having to wait a day or more to get a response from your veterinary surgeon.

All veterinary surgeons are licensed and their diplomas and/or certificates should be displayed in their waiting rooms. There are, however, many veterinary specialities that usually require further studies and internships. There are specialists in heart problems (veterinary cardiologists), skin problems (veterinary dermatologists), teeth and gum problems (veterinary dentists), eye problems (veterinary ophthalmologists), x-rays (veterinary radiologists), and surgeons who have specialities in bones, muscles or other organs. Most veterinary surgeons do routine surgery such as neutering, stitching up wounds and docking tails for those breeds in which such is required for show purposes. When the problem affecting your dog is serious, it is not unusual or impudent to get

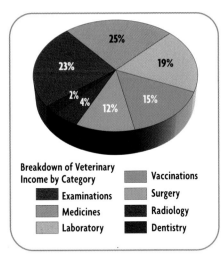

A typical American vet's income, categorised according to services provided. This survey dealt with small-animal practices.

Breakdown of Veterinary Income by Category

- Examinations
- Medicines
- Laboratory
- Vaccinations
- Surgery
- Radiology
- Dentistry

another medical opinion, although in Britain you are obliged to advise the vets concerned about this. You might also want to compare costs among several veterinary surgeons. Sophisticated health care and veterinary services can be very costly. Don't be bashful about discussing these costs with your veterinary surgeon or his (her) staff. Important decisions are often based upon financial considerations.

PREVENTATIVE MEDICINE

It is much easier, less costly and more effective to practise preventative medicine than to fight bouts of illness and disease. Properly bred puppies come from parents that were selected based upon their genetic disease profile. Their mothers should have been vaccinated, free of all internal and

NEUTER OR SPAY

Male dogs are neutered. The operation removes the testicles and requires that the dog be anaesthetised. Recovery takes about one week. Females are spayed. This is major surgery and it usually takes a bitch two weeks to recover.

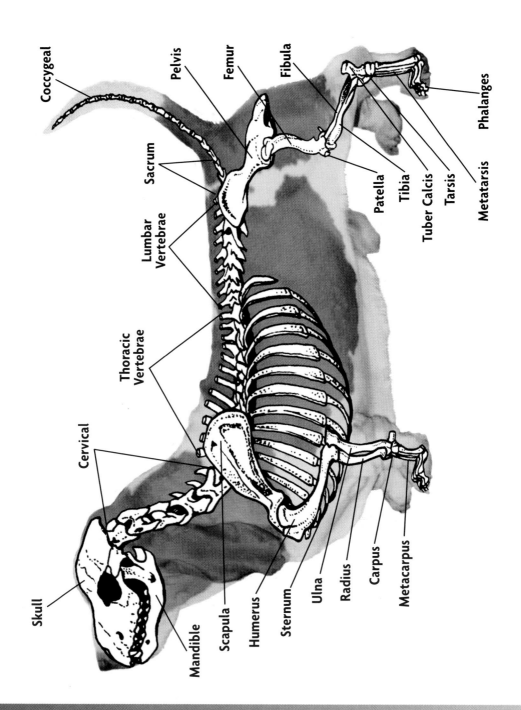

Skeletal Structure of the Basset Hound

Coccygeal

Pelvis

Femur

Fibula

Phalanges

Sacrum

Patella

Tibia

Tuber Calcis

Tarsis

Metatarsis

Lumbar Vertebrae

Thoracic Vertebrae

Cervical

Skull

Mandible

Scapula

Humerus

Sternum

Ulna

Radius

Carpus

Metacarpus

external parasites, and properly nourished. For these reasons, a visit to the veterinary surgeon who cared for the dam (mother) is recommended. The dam can pass on disease resistance to her puppies, which can last for eight to ten weeks. She can also pass on parasites and many infections. That's why you should visit the veterinary surgeon who cared for the dam.

WEANING TO FIVE MONTHS OLD

Puppies should be weaned by the time they are about two months old. A puppy that remains for at least eight weeks with its mother and litter mates usually adapts better to other dogs and people later in its life.

Some new owners have their puppy examined by a veterinary surgeon immediately, which is a good idea. Vaccination

BE CAREFUL WHERE YOUR DOG WALKS

Dogs who have been exposed to lawns sprayed with herbicides have double and triple the rate of malignant lymphoma. Town dogs are especially at risk, as they are exposed to tailored lawns and gardens. Dogs perspire and absorb through their footpads. Be careful where your dog walks and always avoid any area that appears yellowed from chemical overspray.

DENTAL HEALTH

A dental examination is in order when the dog is between six months and one year of age so any permanent teeth that have erupted incorrectly can be corrected. It is important to begin a brushing routine, preferably using a two-sided brushing technique, whereby both sides of the tooth are brushed at the same time. Durable nylon and safe edible chews should be a part of your puppy's arsenal for good health, good teeth and pleasant breath. The vast majority of dogs three to four years old and older have diseases of the gums from lack of dental attention. Using the various types of dental chews can be very effective in controlling dental plaque.

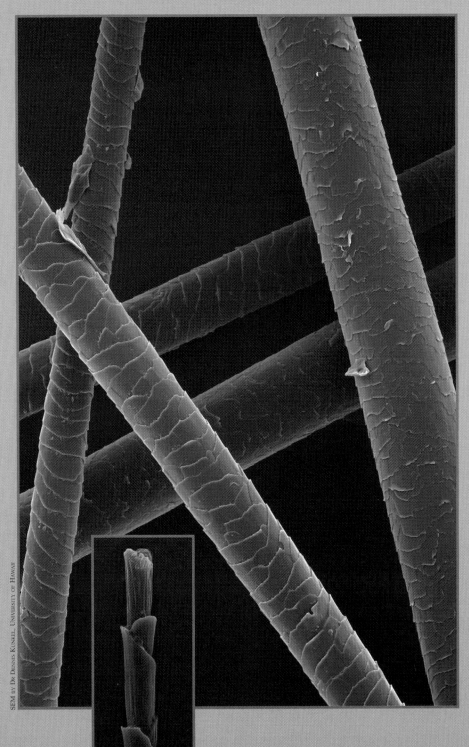

Normal hairs of a dog enlarged 200 times original size. The cuticle (outer covering) is clean and healthy. Unlike human hair that grows from the base, a dog's hair also grows from the end, as shown in the inset. Scanning electron micrographs by Dr Dennis Kunkel, University of Hawaii.

programmes usually begin when the puppy is very young.

The puppy will have its teeth examined and have its skeletal conformation and general health checked prior to certification by the veterinary surgeon. Puppies in certain breeds have problems with their kneecaps, eye cataracts and other eye problems, heart murmurs and undescended testicles. They may also have personality problems and your veterinary surgeon might have training in temperament evaluation.

VACCINATION SCHEDULING

Most vaccinations are given by injection and should only be done by a veterinary surgeon. Both he and you should keep a record of the date of the injection, the identification of the vaccine and the amount given. Some vets give a first vaccination at eight weeks, but most dog breeders prefer the course not to commence until about ten weeks because of negating any antibodies passed on by the dam. The vaccination scheduling is usually based on a 15-day cycle. You must take your vet's advice as to when to vaccinate as this may differ according to the vaccine used. Most vaccinations immunize your puppy against viruses.

The usual vaccines contain immunizing doses of several different viruses such as

VACCINATIONS RECOMMENDED

Your veterinary surgeon will probably recommend that your puppy be vaccinated before you take him outside. There are airborne diseases, parasite eggs in the grass and unexpected visits from other dogs that might be dangerous to your puppy's health.

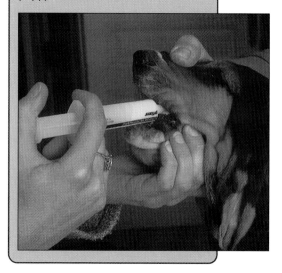

distemper, parvovirus, parainfluenza and hepatitis. There are other vaccines available when the puppy is at risk. You should rely upon professional advice. This is especially true for the booster-shot programme. Most vaccination programmes require a booster when the puppy is a year old and once a year thereafter. In some cases, circumstances may require more or less frequent immunizations.

HEALTH AND VACCINATION SCHEDULE

AGE IN WEEKS:	6TH	8TH	10TH	12TH	14TH	16TH	20-24TH	1 YR
Worm Control	✔	✔	✔	✔	✔	✔	✔	
Neutering								✔
Heartworm*		✔		✔		✔	✔	
Parvovirus	✔		✔		✔		✔	✔
Distemper		✔		✔		✔		✔
Hepatitis		✔		✔		✔		✔
Leptospirosis								✔
Parainfluenza	✔		✔		✔			✔
Dental Examination		✔					✔	✔
Complete Physical		✔					✔	✔
Coronavirus				✔			✔	✔
Kennel Cough	✔							
Hip Dysplasia								✔
Rabies*							✔	

Vaccinations are not instantly effective. It takes about two weeks for the dog's immunization system to develop antibodies. Most vaccinations require annual booster shots. Your veterinary surgeon should guide you in this regard.
*Not applicable in the United Kingdom

Kennel cough, more formally known as tracheobronchitis, is treated with a vaccine that is sprayed into the dog's nostrils. Kennel cough is usually included in routine vaccination, but this is often not so effective as for other major diseases.

FIVE MONTHS TO ONE YEAR OF AGE
Unless you intend to breed or show your dog, neutering the puppy at six months of age is recommended. Discuss this with your veterinary surgeon; most professionals advise neutering the puppy. Neutering has proven to be extremely beneficial to both male and female puppies. Besides eliminating the possibility of pregnancy, it inhibits (but does not prevent) breast cancer in bitches and prostate cancer in male dogs. It is very rare to diagnose breast cancer in a female dog who was spayed at or before about nine months of age.

Your veterinary surgeon should provide your puppy with a thorough dental evaluation at six months of age, ascertaining whether all the permanent teeth have erupted properly. A home dental care regimen should be initiated at six months, including brushing weekly and providing good dental devices (such as nylon bones). Regular dental care promotes healthy teeth, fresh breath and a longer life.

ONE TO SEVEN YEARS
Once a year, your grown dog should visit the vet for an examination and vaccination boosters. Some vets recommend blood tests, thyroid level check and dental evaluation to accompany these annual visits. A thorough clinical evaluation by the vet can provide critical background information for your dog. Blood tests are often performed at one year of age, and dental examinations around the third or fourth birthday. In the long run, quality preventative care for your pet can save money, teeth and lives.

SKIN PROBLEMS IN BASSETS
Veterinary surgeons are consulted by dog owners for skin problems more than any other group of diseases or maladies. Dogs' skin is almost as sensitive as human skin and both suffer almost the same ailments (though the occurrence

DISEASE REFERENCE CHART

	What is it?	What causes it?	Symptoms
Leptospirosis	Severe disease that affects the internal organs; can be spread to people.	A bacterium, which is often carried by rodents, that enters through mucous membranes and spreads quickly throughout the body.	Range from fever, vomiting and loss of appetite in less severe cases to shock, irreversible kidney damage and possibly death in most severe cases.
Rabies	Potentially deadly virus that infects warm-blooded mammals. Not seen in United Kingdom.	Bite from a carrier of the virus, mainly wild animals.	1st stage: dog exhibits change in behaviour, fear. 2nd stage: dog's behaviour becomes more aggressive. 3rd stage: loss of coordination, trouble with bodily functions.
Parvovirus	Highly contagious virus, potentially deadly.	Ingestion of the virus, which is usually spread through the faeces of infected dogs.	Most common: severe diarrhoea. Also vomiting, fatigue, lack of appetite.
Kennel cough	Contagious respiratory infection.	Combination of types of bacteria and virus. Most common: *Bordetella bronchiseptica* bacteria and parainfluenza virus.	Chronic cough.
Distemper	Disease primarily affecting respiratory and nervous system.	Virus that is related to the human measles virus.	Mild symptoms such as fever, lack of appetite and mucous secretion progress to evidence of brain damage, 'hard pad.'
Hepatitis	Virus primarily affecting the liver.	Canine adenovirus type I (CAV-1). Enters system when dog breathes in particles.	Lesser symptoms include listlessness, diarrhoea, vomiting. More severe symptoms include 'blue-eye' (clumps of virus in eye).
Coronavirus	Virus resulting in digestive problems.	Virus is spread through infected dog's faeces.	Stomach upset evidenced by lack of appetite, vomiting, diarrhoea.

12 Ways to Prevent Bloat

Gastric torsion or bloat is a preventable killer of dogs. We know that bloat affects more large dogs and deep-chested dogs than any other dogs. Bloat can be defined as the rapid accumulation of air in the stomach, causing it to twist or flip over, thereby blocking the entrance and exit. A dog suffering from bloat experiences acute pain and is unable to release the gas. Here are some excellent recommendations to prevent this life-threatening condition.

- Do not provide water at mealtimes, especially for dogs that commonly drink large amounts of water
- Keep your dog at his proper weight. Avoid overfeeding.
- Limit exercise one hour before and after mealtime.
- Avoid stressful or vigorous exercise altogether.
- Provide antacids for any dog with audible stomach motions (borborygmus) or flatuelence.
- Feed two or three smaller meals instead of one large meal per day.
- Serve your dog's food on a bowl stand so that he does not have to crane his neck to eat.

- Be certain that mealtime is a non-stressful time. Feed dog alone where he is not competing with a canine or feline housemate for his bowl. Feeding the dog in his crate is an excellent solution.
- For the big gulper, place large toys in the dog's bowl so that he cannot gulp his portions.
- Discuss bloat prevention and preventive surgical methods with your veterinary surgeon.
- If changing your dog's diet, do so gradually.
- Recognise the symptoms of bloat, as time is of the essence. Symptoms include pacing, whining, wretching (with no result), groaning, obvious discomfort.

of acne in dogs is rare!). For this reason, veterinary dermatology has developed into a speciality practised by many veterinary surgeons.

Since many skin problems have visual symptoms that are almost identical, it requires the skill of an experienced veterinary dermatologist to identify and cure many of the more severe skin disorders. Pet shops sell many treatments for skin problems but most of the treatments are directed at symptoms and not the underlying problem(s). If your dog is suffering from a skin disorder, you should seek professional assistance as quickly as possible. As with all diseases, the earlier a

First Aid at a Glance

Burns
Place the affected area under cool water; use ice if only a small area is burnt.

Bee/Insect bites
Apply ice to relieve swelling; antihistamine dosed properly.

Animal bites
Clean any bleeding area; apply pressure until bleeding subsides; go to the vet.

Spider bites
Use cold compress and a pressurised pack to inhibit venom's spreading.

Antifreeze poisoning
Induce vomiting with hydrogen peroxide. Seek *immediate* veterinary help!

Fish hooks
Removal best handled by vet; hook must be cut in order to remove.

Snake bites
Pack ice around bite; contact vet quickly; identify snake for proper antivenin.

Car accident
Move dog from roadway with blanket; seek veterinary aid.

Shock
Calm the dog, keep him warm; seek immediate veterinary help.

Nosebleed
Apply cold compress to the nose; apply pressure to any visible abrasion.

Bleeding
Apply pressure above the area; treat wound by applying a cotton pack.

Heat stroke
Submerge dog in cold bath; cool down with fresh air and water; go to the vet.

Frostbite/Hypothermia
Warm the dog with a warm bath, electric blankets or hot water bottles.

Abrasions
Clean the wound and wash out thoroughly with fresh water; apply antiseptic.

 Remember: an injured dog may attempt to bite a helping hand from fear and confusion. Always muzzle the dog before trying to offer assistance.

problem is identified and treated, the more successful is the cure.

HEREDITARY SKIN DISORDERS

Veterinary dermatologists are currently researching a number of skin disorders that are believed to have a hereditary basis. These inherited diseases are transmitted by both parents, who appear (phenotypically) normal but have a recessive gene for the disease, meaning that they carry, but are not affected by, the disease. These diseases pose serious problems to breeders because in some instances there is no method of identifying carriers. Often the secondary diseases associated with these skin conditions are even more debilitating than the skin disorder, including cancers and respiratory problems; others can be lethal.

Among the known hereditary skin disorders, for which the mode of inheritance is known, are acrodermatitis, cutaneous asthenia (Ehlers-Danlos syndrome), sebaceous adenitis, cyclic hematopoiesis, dermatomyositis, IgA deficiency, colour dilution alopecia and nodular dermatofibrosis. Sebaceous adenitis, while most commonly associated with the Standard Poodle, has also been cited in the Basset Hound. Some of these disorders are limited to one or two breeds and others affect a large number of breeds. All inherited diseases must be diagnosed and treated by a veterinary specialist.

PARASITE BITES

Many of us are allergic to insect bites. The bites itch, erupt and may even become infected. Dogs have the same reaction to fleas, ticks and/or mites. When an insect lands on you, you have the chance to whisk it away with your hand. Unfortunately, when our dog is bitten by a flea, tick or mite, it can only scratch it away or bite it. By the time the dog has been bitten, the parasite has done some of its damage. It may also have laid eggs to cause further problems in the near future. The itching from parasite bites is probably due to the saliva injected into the site when the parasite sucks the dog's blood.

AIRBORNE ALLERGIES

An interesting allergy is pollen allergy. Humans have hay fever, rose fever and other fevers with which they suffer during the pollinating season. Many dogs suffer the same allergies. When the pollen count is high, your dog might suffer but don't expect him to sneeze and have a runny nose like humans. Dogs react to pollen allergies the same way they react to fleas—they scratch and bite themselves.

Dogs, like humans, can be tested for allergens. Discuss the testing with your veterinary dermatologist.

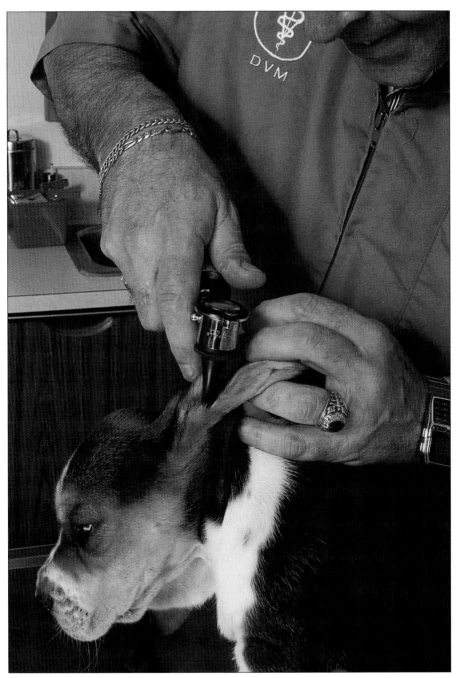

If you select a vet who knows Basset Hounds, he will be familiar with the many problems that can affect the breed, including ears, skin and back problems.

FOOD PROBLEMS

FOOD ALLERGIES

Dogs are allergic to many foods that are best-sellers and highly recommended by breeders and veterinary surgeons. Changing the brand of food that you buy may not eliminate the problem if the element to which the dog is allergic is contained in the new brand.

Recognising a food allergy is difficult. Humans vomit or have rashes when they eat a food to which they are allergic. Dogs neither vomit nor (usually) develop a rash. They react in the same manner as they do to an airborne or flea allergy: they itch, scratch and bite, thus making the diagnosis extremely difficult. While pollen allergies and parasite bites are usually seasonal, food allergies are year-round problems.

FOOD INTOLERANCE

Food intolerance is the inability of the dog to completely digest certain foods. Puppies that may have done very well on their mother's milk may not do well on cow's milk. The result of this food intolerance may be loose bowels, passing gas and stomach pains. These are the only obvious symptoms of food intolerance, which makes diagnosis difficult.

TREATING FOOD PROBLEMS

It is possible to handle food allergies and food intolerance yourself. Put your dog on a diet that it has never had. Obviously if it has never eaten this new food it can't have been allergic or intolerant of it. Start with a single ingredient that is not in the dog's diet at the present time. Ingredients like chopped beef or fish are common in dog's diets, so try something more exotic like rabbit, pheasant or even just vegetables. Keep the dog on this diet (with no additives) for a month. If the symptoms of food allergy or intolerance disappear, chances are your dog has a food allergy.

Don't think that the single ingredient cured the problem. You still must find a suitable diet and ascertain which ingredient in the old diet was objectionable. This is most easily accomplished by adding ingredients to the new diet one at a time. Let the dog stay on the modified diet for a month before you add another ingredient. Eventually, you will determine the ingredient that caused the adverse reaction.

An alternative method is to carefully study the ingredients in the diet to which your dog is allergic or intolerant. Identify the main ingredient in this diet and eliminate the main ingredient by buying a different food that does not have that ingredient. Keep experimenting until the symptoms disappear after one month on the new diet.

Recognising a Sick Dog

Unlike colicky babies and cranky children, our canine kids cannot tell us when they are feeling ill. Therefore, there are a number of signs that owners can identify to know that their dogs are not feeling well.

Take note for physical manifestations such as:

- unusual, bad odour, including bad breath
- excessive moulting
- wax in the ears, chronic ear irritation
- oily, flaky, dull haircoat
- mucous, tearing or similar discharge in the eyes
- fleas or mites
- mucous in stool, diarrhoea
- sensitivity to petting or handling
- licking at paws, scratching face, etc.

Keep an eye out for behavioural changes as well including:

- lethargy, idleness
- lack of patience or general irritability
- lack of appetite, digestive problems
- phobias (fear of people, loud noises, etc.)
- strange behaviour, suspicion, fear
- coprophagia
- more frequent barking
- whimpering, crying

Get Well Soon

You don't need a DVR or a BVMA to provide good TLC to your sick or recovering dog, but you do need to pay attention to some details that normally wouldn't bother him. The following tips will aid Fido's recovery and get him back on his paws again:

- Keep his space free of irritating smells, like heavy perfumes and air fresheners.
- Rest is the best medicine! Avoid harsh lighting that will prevent your dog from sleeping. Shade him from bright sunlight during the day and dim the lights in the evening.
- Keep the noise level down. Animals are more sensitive to sound when they are sick.

- Be attentive to any necessary temperature adjustments. A dog with a fever needs a cool room and cold liquids. A bitch that is whelping or recovering from surgery will be more comfortable in a warm room, consuming warm liquids and food.
- You wouldn't send a sick child back to school early, so don't rush your dog back into a full routine until he seems absolutely ready.

A scanning electron micrograph (S. E. M.) of a dog flea, *Ctenocephalides canis.*

S. E. M. BY DR DENNIS KINKEL, UNIVERSITY OF HAWAII

Magnified head of a dog flea, *Ctenocephalides canis.*

S. E. M. BY DR DENNIS KINKEL, UNIVERSITY OF HAWAII

A male dog flea, *Ctenocephalides canis.*

EXTERNAL PARASITES

Of all the problems to which dogs are prone, none is more well known and frustrating than fleas. Flea infestation is relatively simple to cure but difficult to prevent. Parasites that are harboured inside the body are a bit more difficult to eradicate but they are easier to control.

FLEAS

To control a flea infestation you have to understand the flea's life cycle. Fleas are often thought of as a summertime problem but centrally heated homes have changed the patterns and fleas can be found at any time of the year. The most effective method of flea control is a two-stage approach:

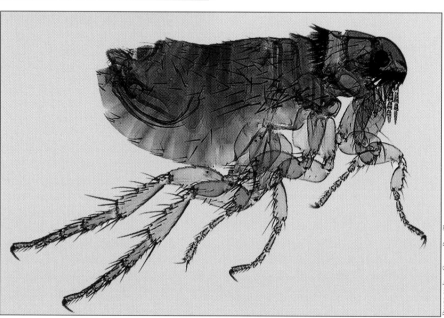

PHOTO BY JEAN CLAUDE REVY/PHOTOTAKE.

FLEA-KILLERS

Flea-killers are poisonous. You should not spray these toxic chemicals on areas of a dog's body that he licks, on his genitals or on his face. Flea killers taken internally are a better answer, but check with your vet in case internal therapy is not advised for your dog.

one stage to kill the adult fleas, and the other to control the development of pre-adult fleas. Unfortunately, no single active ingredient is effective against all stages of the life cycle.

LIFE CYCLE STAGES

During its life, a flea will pass through four life stages: egg, larva, pupa and adult. The adult stage is the most visible and irritating stage of the flea life cycle and this is why the majority of flea-control products concentrate on this stage. The fact is that adult fleas account for only 1% of the total flea population, and the other 99% exist in pre-adult stages, i.e. eggs, larvae and pupae. The pre-adult stages are barely visible to the naked eye.

THE LIFE CYCLE OF THE FLEA

Eggs are laid on the dog, usually in quantities of about 20 or 30, several times a day. The female adult flea must have a blood meal

before each egg-laying session. When first laid, the eggs will cling to the dog's fur, as the eggs are still moist. However, they will quickly dry out and fall from the dog, especially if the dog moves around or scratches. Many eggs will fall off in the dog's favourite area or an area in which he spends a lot of time, such as his bed.

Once the eggs fall from the dog onto the carpet or furniture, they will hatch into larvae. This takes from one to ten days. Larvae are not particularly mobile, and will usually travel only a few inches from where they hatch. However, they do have a tendency to move

A Look at Fleas

Fleas have been around for millions of years and have adapted to changing host animals.
They are able to go through a complete life cycle in less than one month or they can extend their lives to almost two years by remaining as pupae or cocoons. They do not need blood or any other food for up to 20 months.
They have been measured as being able to jump 300,000 times and can jump 150 times their length in any direction including straight up. Those are just a few of the reasons why they are so successful in infesting a dog!

ILLUSTRATION COURTESY OF BAYER VITAL GMBH & CO. KG

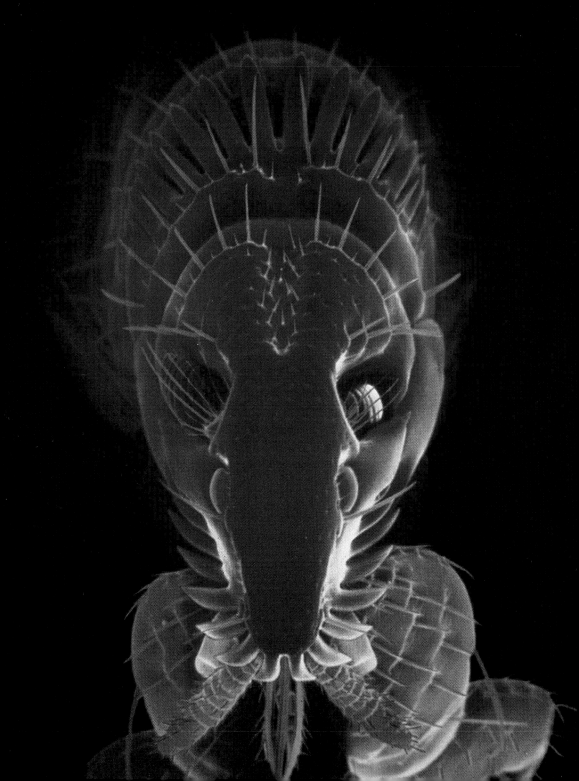

away from light and heavy traffic—under furniture and behind doors are common places to find high quantities of flea larvae.

The flea larvae feed on dead organic matter, including adult flea faeces, until they are ready to change into adult fleas. Fleas will usually remain as larvae for around seven days. After this period, the larvae will pupate into protective pupae. While inside the pupae, the larvae will undergo metamorphosis and change into adult fleas. This can take as little time as a few days, but the adult fleas can remain inside the pupae waiting to hatch for up to two years. The pupae are signalled to hatch by certain stimuli, such as physical pressure—the pupae's being stepped on, heat from an animal lying on the pupae or increased carbon dioxide levels and vibrations—indicating that a suitable host is available.

Once hatched, the adult flea must feed within a few days. Once the adult flea finds a host, it will not leave voluntarily. It only becomes dislodged by grooming or

MIXING CAN BE TOXIC
Never mix flea control products without first consulting your veterinary surgeon. Some products can become toxic when combined with others and can cause serious or fatal consequences.

EN GARDE: CATCHING FLEAS OFF GUARD
Consider the following ways to arm yourself against fleas:
- Add a small amount of pennyroyal or eucalyptus oil to your dog's bath. These natural remedies repel fleas.
- Supplement your dog's food with fresh garlic (minced or grated) and a hearty amount of brewer's yeast, both of which ward off fleas.
- Use a flea comb on your dog daily. Submerge fleas in a cup of bleach to kill them quickly.
- Confine the dog to only a few rooms to limit the spread of fleas in the home.
- Vacuum daily . . . and get all of the crevices! Dispose of the bag every few days until the problem is under control.
- Wash your dog's bedding daily. Cover cushions where your dog sleeps with towels, and wash the towels often.

the host animal's scratching. The adult flea will remain on the host for the duration of its life unless forcibly removed.

TREATING THE ENVIRONMENT AND THE DOG
Treating fleas should be a two-pronged attack. First, the environment needs to be treated; this includes carpets and furniture, especially the dog's bedding and

Opposite page: A scanning electron micrograph of a dog or cat flea, *Ctenocephalides*, magnified more than 100x. This image has been colourised for effect.

The Life Cycle of the Flea

Adult

Pupa

Larva

Egg

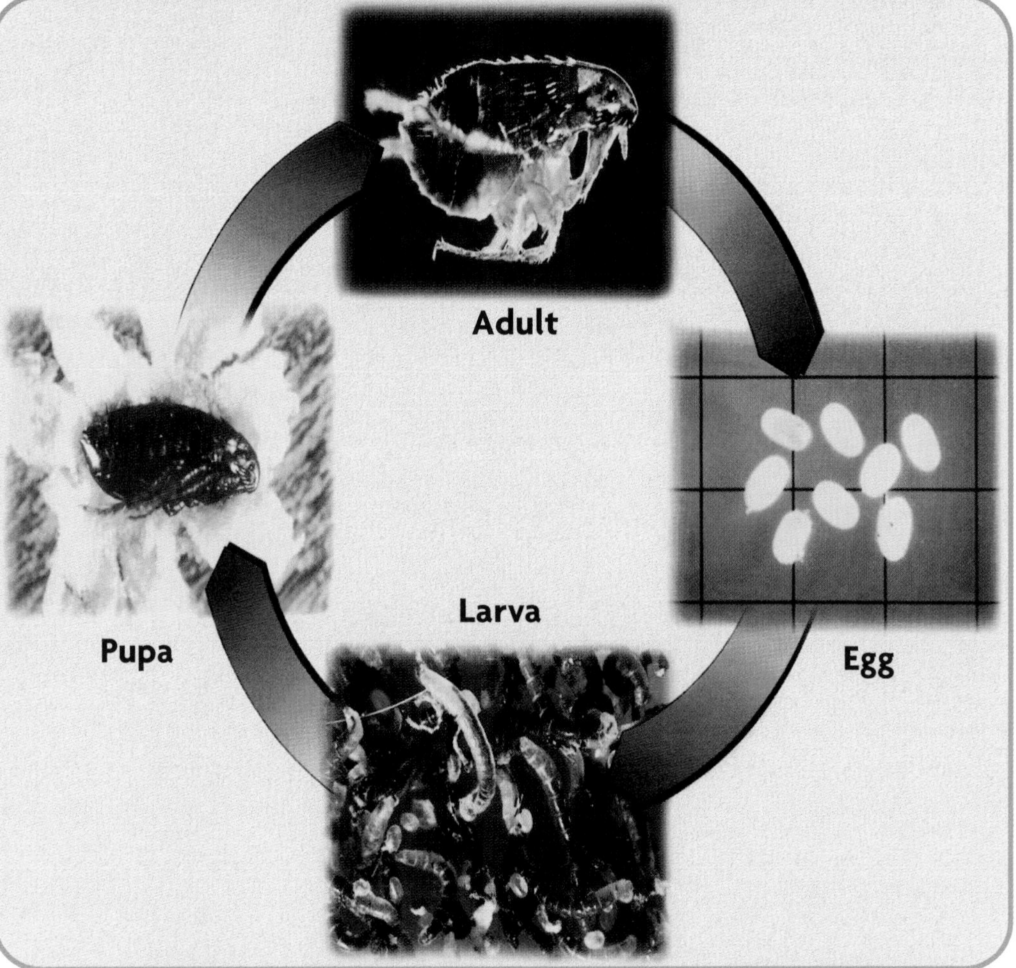

This graphic depiction of the life cycle of the flea appears courtesy of Fleabusters®, R$_x$ for Fleas.

areas underneath furniture. The environment should be treated with a household spray containing an Insect Growth Regulator (IGR) and an insecticide to kill the adult fleas. Most IGRs are effective against eggs and larvae; they actually mimic the fleas' own hormones and stop the eggs and larvae from developing into adult fleas. There are currently no treatments available to attack the pupa stage of the life cycle, so the adult insecticide is used to kill the newly hatched adult fleas before

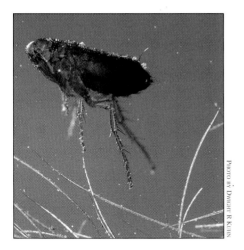

Photo by Dwight R Kuhn

TICKS AND MITES

Though not as common as fleas, ticks and mites are found all over the tropical and temperate world. They don't bite, like fleas; they harpoon. They dig their sharp proboscis (nose) into the dog's skin and drink the blood. Their only food and drink is dog's blood. Dogs can get Lyme disease, Rocky Mountain spotted fever (normally

Dwight R Kuhn's magnificent action photo showing a flea jumping from a dog's back.

they find a host. Most IGRs are active for many months, whilst adult insecticides are only active for a few days.

When treating with a household spray, it is a good idea to vacuum before applying the product. This stimulates as many pupae as possible to hatch into adult fleas. The vacuum cleaner should also be treated with a flea treatment to prevent the eggs and larvae that have been hoovered into the vacuum bag from hatching. The second stage of treatment is to apply an adult insecticide to the dog. Traditionally, this would be in the form of a collar or a spray, but more recent innovations include digestible insecticides that poison the fleas when they ingest the dog's blood. Alternatively, there are drops that, when placed on the back of the animal's neck, spread throughout the fur and skin to kill adult fleas.

FLEA CONTROL

Two types of products should be used when treating fleas—a product to treat the pet and a product to treat the home. Adult fleas represent less than 1% of the flea population. The pre-adult fleas (eggs, larvae and pupae) represent more than 99% of the flea population and are found in the environment; it is in the case of pre-adult fleas that products containing an Insect Growth Regulator (IGR) should be used in the home.

IGRs are a new class of compounds used to prevent the development of insects. They do not kill the insect outright, but instead use the insect's biology against it to stop it from completing its growth. Products that contain methoprene are the world's first and leading IGRs. Used to control fleas and other insects, this type of IGR will stop flea larvae from developing and protect the house for up to seven months.

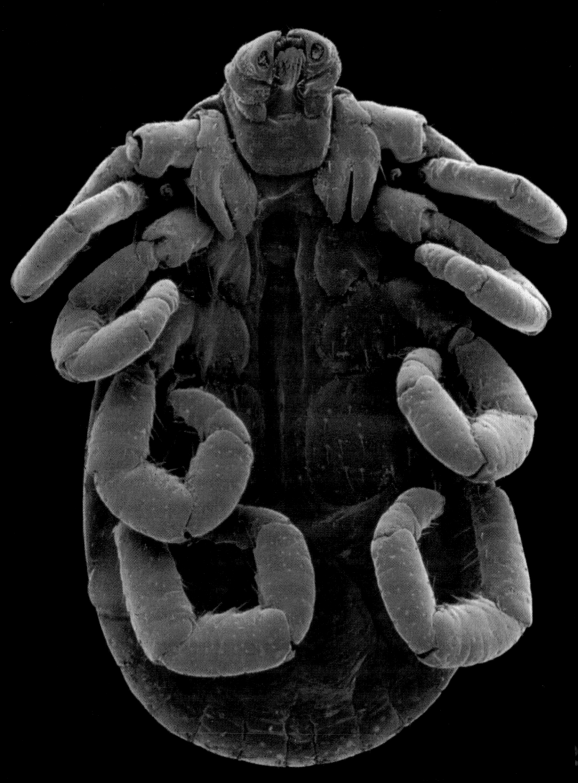

found in the US only), paralysis and many other diseases from ticks and mites. They may live where fleas are found and they like to hide in cracks or seams in walls wherever dogs live. They are controlled the same way fleas are controlled. The dog tick, *Dermacentor variabilis*, may well be the most common dog tick in many geographical areas, especially those areas where the climate is hot and humid.

Most dog ticks have life expectancies of a week to six

Beware the Deer Tick

The great outdoors may be fun for your dog, but it also is a home to dangerous ticks. Deer ticks carry a bacterium known as *Borrelia burgdorferi* and are most active in the autumn and spring. When infections are caught early, penicillin and tetracycline are effective antibiotics, but if left untreated the bacteria may cause neurological, kidney and cardiac problems as well as long-term trouble with walking and painful joints.

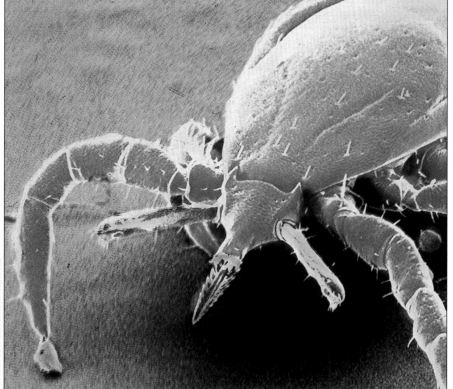

A deer tick, the carrier of Lyme disease. This magnified micrograph has been colourized for effect.

Opposite page: The dog tick, *Dermacentor variabilis*, is probably the most common tick found on dogs. Look at the strength in its eight legs! No wonder it's hard to detach them.

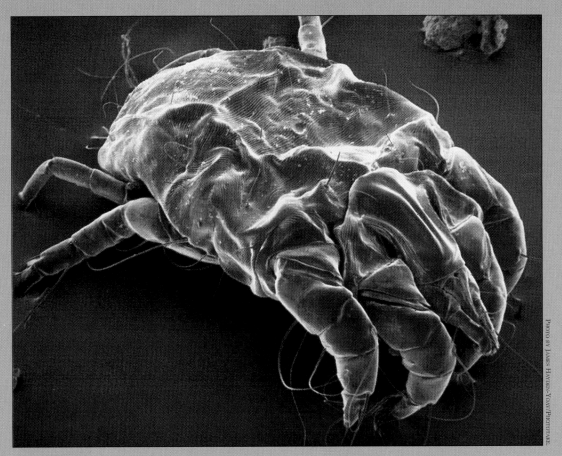

Photo by James Hayden-Yoav/Phototake.

Above:
The mange mite,
Psoroptes bovis.

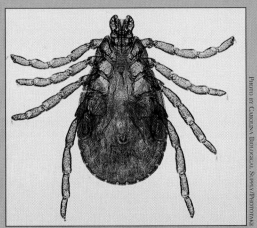

Photo by Carolina Biological Supply/Phototake

A brown dog tick, *Rhipicephalus sanguineus*, is an
uncommon but annoying tick found on dogs.

Photo by Dwight R Kuhn

Human lice look like dog lice;
the two are closely related.

months, depending upon climatic conditions. They can neither jump nor fly, but they can crawl slowly and can range up to 5 metres (16 feet) to reach a sleeping or unsuspecting dog.

MANGE

Mites cause a skin irritation called mange. Some are contagious, like *Cheyletiella*, ear mites, scabies and chiggers. Mites that cause ear-mite infestations are usually controlled with Lindane, which can only be administered by a vet, followed by Tresaderm at home.

It is essential that your dog be treated for mange as quickly as possible because some forms of mange are transmissible to people.

INTERNAL PARASITES

Most animals—fishes, birds and mammals, including dogs and humans—have worms and other parasites that live inside their bodies. According to Dr Herbert R Axelrod, the fish pathologist, there are two kinds of parasites: dumb and smart. The smart parasites live in peaceful cooper-ation with their hosts (symbiosis), while the dumb parasites kill their host. Most of the worm infections are relatively easy to control. If they are not controlled they weaken the host dog to the point that other medical problems occur, but they are not dumb parasites.

ROUNDWORMS

The roundworms that infect dogs are scientifically known as *Toxocara canis*. They live in the dog's intestine. The worms shed eggs continually. It has been estimated that a dog produces about 150 grammes of faeces every day. Each gramme of faeces averages 10,000–12,000 eggs of roundworms. There are no known areas in which dogs roam that do not contain roundworm eggs. The greatest danger of roundworms is that they infect people too! It is

---

DEWORMING

Ridding your puppy of worms is VERY IMPORTANT because certain worms that puppies carry, such as tapeworms and roundworms, can infect humans.

Breeders initiate a deworming programme at or about four weeks of age. The routine is repeated every two or three weeks until the puppy is three months old. The breeder from whom you obtained your puppy should provide you with the complete details of the deworming programme.

Your veterinary surgeon can prescribe and monitor the programme of deworming for you. The usual programme is treating the puppy every 15–20 days until the puppy is positively worm free.

It is advised that you only treat your puppy with drugs that are recommended professionally.

wise to have your dog tested regularly for roundworms.

Pigs also have roundworm infections that can be passed to humans and dogs. The typical roundworm parasite is called *Ascaris lumbricoides*.

HOOKWORMS

The worm *Ancylostoma caninum* is commonly called the dog hookworm. It is dangerous to humans and cats. It also has teeth by which it attaches itself to the intestines of the dog. It changes the site of its attachment about six times a day and the dog loses blood from each detachment, possibly causing iron-deficiency anaemia. Hookworms are easily purged from the dog with many medications. Milbemycin oxime,

ROUNDWORM

Average size dogs can pass 1,360,000 roundworm eggs every day.

For example, if there were only 1 million dogs in the world, the world would be saturated with 1,300 metric tonnes of dog faeces.

These faeces would contain 15,000,000,000 roundworm eggs.

It's known that 7–31% of home gardens and children's play boxes in the US contain roundworm eggs.

Flushing dog's faeces down the toilet is not a safe practice because the usual sewage treatments do not destroy roundworm eggs.

Infected puppies start shedding roundworm eggs at 3 weeks of age. They can be infected by their mother's milk.

The roundworm, *Rhabditis*. The roundworm can infect both dogs and humans.

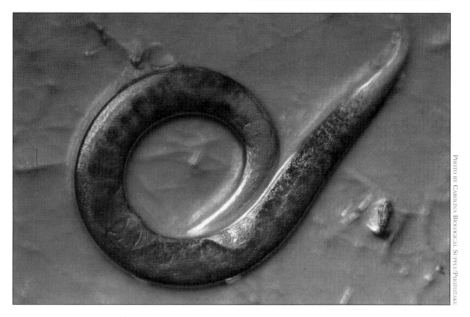

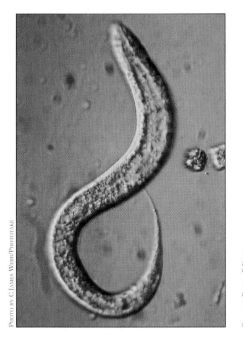

PHOTO BY C JAMES WEBB/PHOTOTAKE

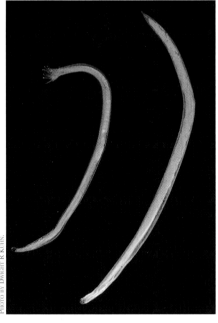

PHOTO BY DWIGHT R KUHN

Left:
The infective stage of the hookworm larva.

Right:
Male and female hookworms, *Ancylostoma caninum*, are uncommonly found in pet or show dogs in Britain. Hookworms may infect other dogs that have exposure to grasslands.

which also serves as a heartworm preventative in Collies, can be used for this purpose.

In Britain the 'temperate climate' hookworm (*Uncinaria stenocephala*) is rarely found in pet or show dogs, but can occur in

CAUTION: NO SWIMMING!

Never allow your dog to swim in polluted water or public areas where water quality can be suspect. Even perfectly clear water can harbour parasites, many of which can cause serious to fatal illnesses in canines. Areas inhabited by waterfowl and other wildlife are especially dangerous.

hunting packs, racing Greyhounds and sheepdogs because the worms can be prevalent wherever dogs are exercised regularly on grassland.

TAPEWORMS

There are many species of tapeworms. They are carried by fleas! The dog eats the flea and starts the tapeworm cycle. Humans can also be infected with tapeworms, so don't eat fleas! Fleas are so small that your dog could pass them onto your hands, your plate or your food and thus make it possible for you to ingest a flea which is carrying tapeworm eggs.

While tapeworm infection is not life threatening in dogs (smart parasite!), it can be the cause of a

135

The head and rostellum (the round prominence on the scolex) of a tapeworm, which infects dogs and humans.

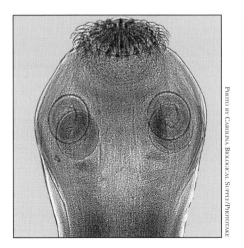

PHOTO BY CAROLINA BIOLOGICAL SUPPLY/PHOTOTAKE

very serious liver disease for humans. About 50 percent of the humans infected with *Echinococcus multilocularis*, a type of tapeworm that causes alveolar hydatis, perish.

HEARTWORMS

Heartworms are thin, extended worms up to 30 cms (12 ins) long which live in a dog's heart and the major blood vessels surrounding it. Dogs may have up to 200 worms. Symptoms may be loss of energy, loss of appetite, coughing, the development of a pot belly and anaemia.

Heartworms are transmitted by mosquitoes. The mosquito drinks the blood of an infected dog and takes in larvae with the blood. The larvae, called microfilaria, develop within the body of the mosquito and are passed on to the next dog bitten after the larvae mature. It takes two to three weeks for the

TAPEWORM

Humans, rats, squirrels, foxes, coyotes, wolves, mixed breeds of dogs and purebred dogs are all susceptible to tapeworm infection. Except in humans, tapeworms are usually not a fatal infection.

Infected individuals can harbour a thousand parasitic worms.

Tapeworms have two sexes—male and female (many other worms have only one sex—male and female in the same worm).

If dogs eat infected rats or mice, they get the tapeworm disease.

One month after attaching to a dog's intestine, the worm starts shedding eggs. These eggs are infective immediately.

Infective eggs can live for a few months without a host animal.

Roundworms, whipworms and hookworms are just a few of the other commonly known worms that infect dogs.

larvae to develop to the infective stage within the body of the mosquito. Dogs should be treated at about six weeks of age, and maintained on a prophylactic dose given monthly.

Blood testing for heartworms is not necessarily indicative of how seriously your dog is infected. This is a dangerous disease. Although heartworm is a problem for dogs in America, Australia, Asia and Central Europe, dogs in the United Kingdom are not currently affected by heartworm.

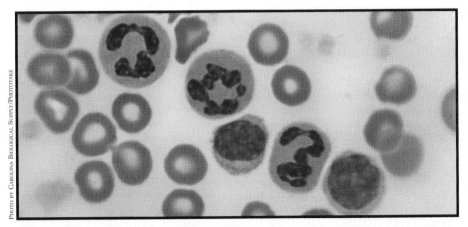

Magnified heartworm larvae, *Dirofilaria immitis.*

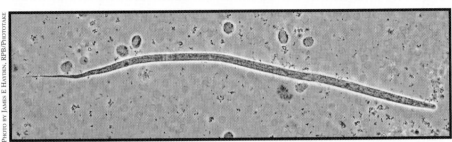

The heartworm, *Dirofilaria immitis.*

The heart of a dog infected with canine heartworm, *Dirofilaria immitis.*

137

HOMEOPATHY:
an alternative to conventional medicine

'Less is Most'

Using this principle, the strength of a homeopathic remedy is measured by the number of serial dilutions that were undertaken to create it. The greater the number of serial dilutions, the greater the strength of the homeopathic remedy. The potency of a remedy that has been made by making a dilution of 1 part in 100 parts (or 1/100) is 1c or 1cH. If this remedy is subjected to a series of further dilutions, each one being 1/100, a more dilute and stronger remedy is produced. If the remedy is diluted in this way six times, it is called 6c or 6cH. A dilution of 6c is 1 part in 1000,000,000,000. In general, higher potencies in more frequent doses are better for acute symptoms and lower potencies in more infrequent doses are more useful for chronic, long-standing problems.

CURING OUR DOGS NATURALLY

Holistic medicine means treating the whole animal as a unique, perfect living being. Generally, holistic treatments do not suppress the symptoms that the body naturally produces, as do most medications prescribed by conventional doctors and vets. Holistic methods seek to cure disease by regaining balance and harmony in the patient's environment. Some of these methods include use of nutritional therapy, herbs, flower essences, aromatherapy, acupuncture, massage, chiropractic, and, of course the most popular holistic approach, homeopathy. Homeopathy is a theory or system of treating illness with small doses of substances which, if administered in larger quantities, would produce the symptoms that the patient already has. This approach is often described as 'like cures like.' Although modern veterinary medicine is geared toward the 'quick fix,' homeopathy relies on the belief that, given the time, the body is able to heal itself and return to its natural, healthy state.

Choosing a remedy to cure a problem in our dogs is the difficult part of homeopathy. Consult with your veterinary surgeon for a professional diagnosis of your dog's symptoms. Often these symptoms require immediate conventional

care. If your vet is willing, and somewhat knowledgeable, you may attempt a homeopathic remedy. Be aware that cortisone prevents homeopathic remedies from working. There are hundreds of possibilities and combinations to cure many problems in dogs, from basic physical problems such as excessive moulting, fleas or other parasites, unattractive doggy odour, bad breath, upset tummy, dry, oily or dull coat, diarrhoea, ear problems or eye discharge (including tears and dry or mucousy matter), to behavioural abnormalities, such as fear of loud noises, habitual licking, poor appetite, excessive barking, obesity and various phobias. From alumina to zincum metallicum, the remedies span the planet and the imagination…from flowers and weeds to chemicals, insect droppings, diesel smoke and volcanic ash.

Using 'Like to Treat Like'

Unlike conventional medicines that suppress symptoms, homeopathic remedies treat illnesses with small doses of substances that, if administered in larger quantities, would produce the symptoms that the patient already has. Whilst the same homeopathic remedy can be used to treat different symptoms in different dogs, here are some interesting remedies and their uses.

Apis Mellifica
(made from honey bee venom) can be used for allergies or to reduce swelling that occurs in acutely infected kidneys.

Diesel Smoke
can be used to help control travel sickness.

Calcarea Fluorica
(made from calcium fluoride which helps harden bone structure) can be useful in treating hard lumps in tissues.

Natrum Muriaticum
(made from common salt, sodium chloride) is useful in treating thin, thirsty dogs.

Nitricum Acidum
(made from nitric acid) is used for symptoms you would expect to see from contact with acids such as lesions, especially where the skin joins the linings of body orifices or openings such as the lips and nostrils.

Symphytum
(made from the herb Knitbone, Symphytum officianale) is used to encourage bones to heal.

Urtica Urens
(made from the common stinging nettle) is used in treating painful, irritating rashes.

HOMEOPATHIC REMEDIES FOR YOUR DOG

Symptom/Ailment	Possible Remedy
ALLERGIES	Apis Mellifica 30c, Astacus Fluviatilis 6c, Pulsatilla 30c, Urtica Urens 6c
ALOPECIA	Alumina 30c, Lycopodium 30c, Sepia 30c, Thallium 6c
ANAL GLANDS (BLOCKED)	Hepar Sulphuris Calcareum 30c, Sanicula 6c, Silicea 6c
ARTHRITIS	Rhus Toxicodendron 6c, Bryonia Alba 6c
CATARACT	Calcarea Carbonica 6c, Conium Maculatum 6c, Phosphorus 30c, Silicea 30c
CONSTIPATION	Alumina 6c, Carbo Vegetabilis 30c, Graphites 6c, Nitricum Acidum 30c, Silicea 6c
COUGHING	Aconitum Napellus 6c, Belladonna 30c, Hyoscyamus Niger 30c, Phosphorus 30c
DIARRHOEA	Arsenicum Album 30c, Aconitum Napellus 6c, Chamomilla 30c, Mercurius Corrosivus 30c
DRY EYE	Zincum Metallicum 30c
EAR PROBLEMS	Aconitum Napellus 30c, Belladonna 30c, Hepar Sulphuris 30c, Tellurium 30c, Psorinum 200c
EYE PROBLEMS	Borax 6c, Aconitum Napellus 30c, Graphites 6c, Staphysagria 6c, Thuja Occidentalis 30c
GLAUCOMA	Aconitum Napellus 30c, Apis Mellifica 6c, Phosphorus 30c
HEAT STROKE	Belladonna 30c, Gelsemium Sempervirens 30c, Sulphur 30c
HICCOUGHS	Cinchona Deficinalis 6c
HIP DYSPLASIA	Colocynthis 6c, Rhus Toxicodendron 6c, Bryonia Alba 6c
INCONTINENCE	Argentum Nitricum 6c, Causticum 30c, Conium Maculatum 30c, Pulsatilla 30c, Sepia 30c
INSECT BITES	Apis Mellifica 30c, Cantharis 30c, Hypericum Perforatum 6c, Urtica Urens 30c
ITCHING	Alumina 30c, Arsenicum Album 30c, Carbo Vegetabilis 30c, Hypericum Perforatum 6c, Mezerium 6c, Sulphur 30c
KENNEL COUGH	Drosera 6c, Ipecacuanha 30c
MASTITIS	Apis Mellifica 30c, Belladonna 30c, Urtica Urens 1m
PATELLAR LUXATION	Gelsemium Sempervirens 6c, Rhus Toxicodendron 6c
PENIS PROBLEMS	Aconitum Napellus 30c, Hepar Sulphuris Calcareum 30c, Pulsatilla 30c, Thuja Occidentalis 6c
PUPPY TEETHING	Calcarea Carbonica 6c, Chamomilla 6c, Phytolacca 6c
TRAVEL SICKNESS	Cocculus 6c, Petroleum 6c

CDS
COGNITIVE DYSFUNCTION SYNDROME
'Old Dog Syndrome'

SYMPTOMS OF CDS

There are many ways to evaluate old-dog syndrome. Veterinary surgeons have defined CDS (cognitive dysfunction syndrome) as the gradual deterioration of cognitive abilities. These are indicated by changes in the dog's behaviour. When a dog changes its routine response, and maladies have been eliminated as the cause of these behavioural changes, then CDS is the usual diagnosis.

More than half the dogs over 8 years old suffer some form of CDS. The older the dog, the more chance it has of suffering from CDS. In humans, doctors often dismiss the CDS behavioural changes as part of 'winding down.'

There are four major signs of CDS: frequent toilet accidents inside the home, sleeps much more or much less than normal, acts confused, and fails to respond to social stimuli.

FREQUENT TOILET ACCIDENTS
- *Urinates in the house.*
- *Defecates in the house.*
- *Doesn't signal that he wants to go out.*

SLEEP PATTERNS
- *Moves much more slowly.*
- *Sleeps more than normal during the day.*
- *Sleeps less during the night.*

CONFUSION
- *Goes outside and just stands there.*
- *Appears confused with a faraway look in his eyes.*
- *Hides more often.*
- *Doesn't recognise friends.*
- *Doesn't come when called.*
- *Walks around listlessly and without a destination goal.*

FAILS TO RESPOND TO SOCIAL STIMULI
- *Comes to people less frequently, whether called or not.*
- *Doesn't tolerate petting for more than a short time.*
- *Doesn't come to the door when you return home from work.*

The term *old* is a qualitative term. For dogs, as well as their masters, old is relative. Certainly we can all distinguish between a puppy Basset and an adult Basset—there are the obvious physical traits, such as size, appearance and facial expressions, and personality traits. Puppies that are nasty are very rare. Puppies and young dogs like to play with children. Children's natural exuberance is a good match for the seemingly endless energy of young dogs. They like to run, jump, chase and retrieve. When dogs grow up and cease their interaction with children, they are often thought of as being too old to play with the kids.

On the other hand, if a Basset is only exposed to people over 60 years of age, its life will normally be less active and it will not seem to be getting old as its activity level slows down.

If people live to be 100 years old, dogs live to be 20 years old. While this is a good rule of thumb, it is very inaccurate. When trying to compare dog years to human years, you cannot make a generalisation about all dogs. You can make the generalisation that 12 years is a good lifespan for a Basset, but you cannot compare it to that of a Chihuahua as many toy breeds typically live longer, 15 years is not unusual, or to giant breeds, such as the St. Bernard, which typically live 7 to 9 years. Dogs are generally considered mature within three years, but they can reproduce even earlier. So the first three years of a dog's life are like seven times that of comparable humans. That means a 3-year-old dog is like a 21-year-old human. As the curve of comparison shows, there is no hard and fast rule for comparing dog and human ages. The comparison is made even more difficult, for not all humans age at the same rate...and human females live longer than human males.

When Your Dog Gets Old...
Signs the Owner Can Look For

IF YOU NOTICE...	IT COULD INDICATE...
Discoloration of teeth and gums, foul breath, loss of appetite	Abcesses, gum disease, mouth lesions
Lumps, bumps, cysts, warts, fatty tumours	Cancers, benign or malignant
Cloudiness of eyes, apparent loss of sight	Cataracts, lenticular sclerosis, PRA, retinal dysplasia, blindness
Flaky coat, alopaecia (hair loss)	Hormonal problems, hypothyroidism
Obesity, appetite loss, excessive weight gain	Various problems
Household accidents, increased urination	Diabetes, kidney or bladder disease
Increased thirst	Kidney disease, diabetes mellitus
Change in sleeping habits, coughing	Heart disease
Difficulty moving	Arthritis, degenerative joint disease, spondylosis (degenerative spine disease)

If you notice any of these signs, an appointment should be made immediately with a veterinary surgeon for a thorough evaluation.

DID YOU KNOW?

Your senior dog may lose interest in eating, not because he's less hungry but because his senses of smell and taste have diminished. The old chow simply does not smell as good as it once did. Additionally, older dogs use less energy and thereby can sustain themselves on less food.

WHAT TO LOOK FOR IN SENIORS

Most veterinary surgeons and behaviourists use the seventh year mark as the time to consider a dog a 'senior.' The term 'senior' does not imply that the dog is geriatric and has begun to fail in mind and body. Ageing is essentially a slowing process. Humans readily admit that they feel a difference in their activity level from age 20 to 30, and then from 30 to 40, etc. By treating the seven-year-old dog as a senior, owners are able to implement certain therapeutic and preventative medical strategies with the help of their veterinary surgeons. A senior-care programme should include at least two veterinary visits per year, screening sessions to determine the dog's health status, as well as nutritional counselling. Veterinary surgeons determine the senior dog's health status through a blood smear for a complete blood count, serum chemistry profile with electrolytes, urinalysis, blood pressure check, electrocardiogram, ocular tonometry (pressure on the eyeball) and dental prophylaxis.

Such an extensive programme for senior dogs is well advised before owners start to see the obvious physical

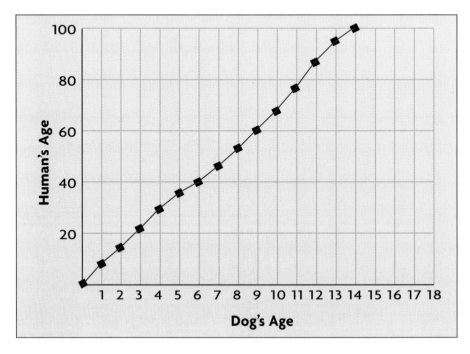

signs of ageing, such as slower and inhibited movement, greying, increased sleep/nap periods and disinterest in play and other activity. This preventative programme promises a longer, healthier life for the ageing dog. Among the physical problems common in ageing dogs are the loss of sight and hearing, arthritis, kidney and liver failure, diabetes mellitus, heart disease and Cushing's disease (a hormonal disease).

In addition to the physical manifestations discussed, there are some behavioural changes and problems related to ageing dogs. Dogs suffering from hearing or vision loss, dental discomfort or arthritis can become aggressive. Likewise the near-deaf and/or blind dog may be startled more easily and react in an unexpectedly aggressive manner. Seniors suffering from senility can become more impatient and irritable. Housesoiling accidents are associated with loss of mobility, kidney problems and loss of sphincter control as well as plaque accumulation, physiological brain changes and reactions to medications. Older dogs, just like young puppies, suffer from separation anxiety, which can lead to excessive barking, whining, housesoiling and destructive behaviour. Seniors may become fearful of everyday sounds, such as vacuum cleaners, heaters, thunder and passing traffic. Some dogs have difficulty sleeping, due to discomfort, the need for frequent toilet visits and the like.

Owners should avoid spoiling the older dog with too many fatty treats. Obesity, no stranger to the Basset at any age, is a common problem in older dogs and subtracts years from their lifespan. Keep the senior dog as trim as possible since excessive weight puts additional stress on the body's vital organs. Some breeders recommend supplementing the diet with foods high in fibre and lower in calories. Adding fresh vegetables and marrow broth to the senior's diet makes a tasty, low-calorie, low-fat supplement. Vets also offer speciality diets for senior dogs that are worth exploring.

Your dog, as he nears his twilight years, needs his owner's patience and good care more than ever. Never punish an older dog for an accident or abnormal behaviour. For all the years of love, protection and companionship that your dog has provided, he deserves special attention and courtesies. The older dog may need to relieve himself at 3 a.m. because he can no longer hold it for eight hours. Older dogs may

not be able to remain crated for more than two or three hours. It may be time to give up a sofa or chair to your old friend. Although he may not seem as enthusiastic about your attention and petting, he does appreciate the considerations you offer as he gets older.

Your Basset does not understand why his world is slowing down. Owners must make the transition into the golden years as pleasant and rewarding as possible.

WHAT TO DO WHEN THE TIME COMES
You are never fully prepared to make a rational decision about putting your dog to sleep. It is very obvious that you love your Basset or you would not be reading this book. Putting a loved dog to sleep is extremely difficult. It is a decision that

must be made with your veterinary surgeon. You are usually forced to make the decision when one of the life-threatening symptoms listed above becomes serious enough for you to seek medical (veterinary) help.

If the prognosis of the malady indicates the end is near and your beloved pet will only suffer more and experience no enjoyment for the balance of its life, then euthanasia is the right choice.

WHAT IS EUTHANASIA?

Euthanasia derives from the Greek meaning *good death*. In other words, it means the planned, painless killing of a dog suffering from a painful, incurable condition, or who is so aged that it cannot walk, see, eat or control its excretory functions.

Euthanasia is usually accomplished by injection with an overdose of an anaesthesia or barbiturate. Aside from the prick of the needle, the experience is usually painless.

MAKING THE DECISION

The decision to euthanize your dog is never easy. The days during which the dog becomes ill and the end occurs can be unusually stressful for you. If this is your first experience with the death of a loved one, you may need the comfort dictated by your religious beliefs. If you are the head of the family and have children, you should have involved them in the decision of putting your Basset to sleep. Usually your dog can be maintained on drugs for a few days in order to give you ample time to make a decision. During this time, talking with members of your family or even people who have lived through this same experience can ease the burden of your inevitable decision.

147

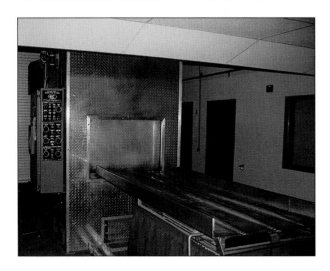

A typical crematorium for small animals.

GETTING ANOTHER DOG?

The grief of losing your beloved dog will be as lasting as the grief of losing a human friend or relative. In most cases, if your dog died of old age (if there is such a thing), it had slowed down considerably. Do you want a new Basset puppy to replace it? Or are you better off

THE FINAL RESTING PLACE

Dogs can have some of the same privileges as humans. The remains of your beloved dog can be buried in a pet cemetery, which is generally expensive. Dogs who have died at home can be buried in your garden in a place suitably marked with some stone or newly planted tree or bush. Alternatively, they can be cremated individually and the ashes returned to you. A less expensive option is mass cremation, although, of course, the ashes can not then be returned. Vets can usually arrange the cremation on your behalf. In Britain if your dog has died at the surgery the vet legally cannot allow you to take your dog's body home. The cost of these options should always be discussed frankly and openly with your veterinary surgeon.

In most crematories there are urns for the ashes. These are usually sold directly or through your veterinary surgeon.

TO THE RESCUE

Some people choose to adopt or 'rescue' older dogs instead of buying a new puppy. Older dogs may have come from abusive environments and be fearful, and some dogs have just developed many bad habits, which can present a challenge to their new owners. Training an older dog will take more time and patience, but persistence and an abundance of praise and love can transform a dog into a well-behaved, loyal companion.

housetrained and will have an already developed personality? In this case, you can find out if you like each other after a few hours of being together.

The decision is, of course, your own. Do you want another Basset or perhaps a different breed so as to avoid comparison with your beloved friend? Most people usually buy the same breed because they know (and love) the characteristics of that breed. Then, too, they often know people who have the same breed and perhaps they are lucky enough that a breeder they know and respect expects a litter soon. What could be better?

in finding a more mature Basset, say two to three years of age, which will usually be

Pet cemeteries exist in most communities. Consult your vet for a facility that he recommends.

When you purchased your Basset Hound you should have made it clear to the breeder whether you wanted one just as a loveable companion and pet, or if you hoped to be buying a Basset with show prospects. No reputable breeder will sell you a young puppy saying that it is *definitely* of show quality, for so much can go wrong during the early weeks and months of a puppy's development. If you plan to show, what you will hopefully have acquired is a puppy with 'show potential.'

To the novice, exhibiting a Basset in the show ring may look easy but it takes a lot of hard work and devotion to do top winning at a show such as the prestigious Crufts Dog Show, not to mention a little luck too!

The first concept that the canine novice learns when watching a dog show is that each dog first competes against members of its own breed. Once the judge has selected the best member of each breed, provided that the show is judged on a Group system, that chosen dog will compete with other dogs in its group. Finally the best of each group will compete for Best in

Show and Reserve Best in Show.

The second concept that you must understand is that the dogs are not actually competing against one another. The judge compares each dog against the breed standard, which is a written description of the ideal specimen of the breed. While some early breed standards were indeed based on specific dogs that were famous or popular, many dedicated enthusiasts say that a perfect specimen, described in the standard, has never been bred. Thus the 'perfect' dog never walked into a show ring and, to the woe of dog breeders around the globe, does not exist. Breeders attempt to get as close to this ideal as possible, with every litter, but theoretically the 'perfect' dog is so elusive that it is impossible. (And if the 'perfect' dog were born, breeders and judges would never agree that it was indeed 'perfect.')

If you are interested in exploring dog shows, your best bet is to join your local breed club. These clubs often host both Championship and Open Shows, and sometimes Match meetings and Special Events, all of which could be of interest, even if you are only an onlooker. Clubs also send out newsletters and some organise training days and seminars in order that people may learn more about their chosen breed. To locate the nearest breed club for you, contact The Kennel Club, the ruling body for the British dog world. The Kennel Club governs not only conformation shows but also working trials, obedience trials, agility trials and field trials. The Kennel Club furnishes the rules and regulations for all these events plus general dog registration and other basic requirements of dog ownership. Its annual show called the Crufts Dog Show, held in Birmingham, is the largest bench show in England. Every year around 20,000 of the UK's best dogs qualify to participate in this marvellous show which lasts four days.

The Kennel Club governs many different kinds of shows in Great Britain, Australia, South Africa and beyond. At the most competitive and prestigious of these shows, the Championship Shows, a dog can earn Challenge Certificates, and thereby become a Show Champion or a Champion. A dog must earn three Challenge Certificates under three different judges to earn the prefix of 'Sh Ch' or 'Ch.' Note that some breeds must also qualify in a field trial in order to gain the title of full

CLUB INFORMATION
You can get information about dog shows from kennel clubs and breed clubs:

Fédération Cynologique Internationale
14, rue Leopold II, B-6530 Thuin, Belgium
www.fci.be

The Kennel Club
1-5 Clarges St., Piccadilly, London W1Y 8AB, UK
www.the-kennel-club.org.uk

American Kennel Club
5580 Centerview Drive
Raleigh, NC 27606-3390, USA
www.akc.org

Canadian Kennel Club
89 Skyway Ave., Suite 100
Etobicoke, Ontario M9W 6R4 Canada
www.ckc.ca

champion. Challenge Certificates (CCs) are awarded to a very small percentage of the dogs competing, especially as dogs which are already Champions compete with others for these coveted CCs. The number of Challenge Certificates awarded in any one year is based upon the total number of dogs in each breed entered for competition. There are three types of Championship Shows: an all-breed General Championship Show for all Kennel Club recognised breeds, a Group Championship Show, limited to breeds within one of the groups, and a Breed Show, usually confined to a single breed. The

Kennel Club determines which breeds at which Championship Shows will have the opportunity to earn CCs (or tickets). Serious exhibitors often will opt not to participate if the tickets are withheld at a particular show. This policy makes earning championships even more difficult to accomplish.

Open Shows are generally less competitive and are frequently used as 'practice shows' for young dogs. There are hundreds of Open Shows each year that can be invitingly social events and are great first show experiences for the novice. Even if you're considering just watching a show to wet your paws, an Open Show is a great choice.

While Championship and Open Shows are most important for the beginner to understand, there are other types of shows in which the interested dog owner can participate. Training clubs sponsor Matches that can be entered on the day of the show for a nominal fee. In these introductory-level exhibitions, two dogs are pulled out of a hat and 'matched,' the winner of that match goes on to the next round, and eventually only one dog is left undefeated.

Exemption Shows are much more light-hearted affairs with usually only four pedigree classes and several 'fun' classes, all of which can be entered on the day. Exemption Shows are sometimes held in conjunction with small agricultural shows and the proceeds must be given to a charity. Limited Shows are also available in small number, but entry is restricted to members of the club which hosts the show, although you can usually join the club when making an entry.

Before you actually step into the ring, you would be well advised to sit back and observe the judge's ring procedure. If it is your first time in the ring, do not be over-anxious and run to the front of the line. It is much better to stand back and study how the exhibitor in front of you is performing. The judge asks each handler to 'stand' the dog, hopefully showing the dog off to his best advantage. The judge will observe the dog from a distance and from different angles, approach the dog, check his teeth, overall structure, alertness and muscle tone, as well as consider how well the dog 'conforms' to the standard. Most importantly, the judge will have the exhibitor move the dog around the ring in some pattern that he or she should specify (another advantage to not going first, but always listen since some judges change their directions, and the judge is always right!) Finally the judge will give the dog one last look before moving

on to the next exhibitor.

If you are not in the top three at your first show, do not be discouraged. Be patient and consistent and you may eventually find yourself in the winning lineup. Remember that the winners were once in your shoes and have devoted many hours and much money to earn the placement. If you find that your dog is losing every time and never getting a nod, it may be time to consider a different dog sport or just enjoy your Basset as a pet.

WORKING TRIALS
Working trials can be entered by any well-trained dog of any breed, not just Gundogs or

Working dogs. Many dogs that earn the Kennel Club Good Citizen Dog award choose to participate in a working trial. There are five stakes at both open and championship levels: Companion Dog (CD), Utility Dog (UD), Working Dog (WD), Tracking Dog (TD) and Patrol Dog (PD). As in conformation shows, dogs compete against a standard and if the dog reaches the qualifying mark, it obtains a certificate. Divided into groups, each exercise must be achieved 70 percent in order to qualify. If the dog achieves 80 percent in the open level, it receives a Certificate of Merit (COM); in the championship level, it receives a Qualifying Certificate. At the CD

A Basset Hound won Group 2 at the 1999 Crufts Dog Show, the most prestigious of dog competitions in Britain. An Elkhound was the Group 1 winner.

FIELD TRIALS AND WORKING TESTS

Working tests are frequently used to prepare dogs for field trials, the purpose of which is to heighten the instincts and natural abilities of Gundogs. Live game is not used in working tests. Unlike field trials, working tests do not count toward a dog's record at The Kennel Club, though the same judges often oversee working tests. Field trials began in England in 1947 and are only moderately popular among dog folk. While breeders of Working and Gundog breeds concern themselves with the field abilities of their dogs, there is considerably less interest in field trials than dog shows. In order for dogs to become full champions, certain breeds must qualify in the field as well. Upon gaining three CCs in

stake, dogs must participate in four groups: Control, Stay, Agility and Search (Retrieve and Nosework). At the next three levels, UD, WD and TD, there are only three groups: Control, Agility and Nosework.

Agility consists of three jumps: a vertical scale up a wall of planks; a clear jump over a basic hurdle with a removable top bar; and a long jump across angled planks. To earn the UD, WD and TD, dogs must track approximately one-half mile for articles laid from one-half hour to three hours ago. Tracks consist of turns and legs, and fresh ground is used for each participant.

The fifth stake, PD, involves teaching manwork, which is not recommended for every breed.

the show ring, the dog is designated a Show Champion (Sh Ch). The title Champion (Ch) requires that the dog gain an award at a field trial, be a 'special qualifier' at a field trial or pass a 'special show dog qualifier' judged by a field trial judge on a shooting day.

AGILITY TRIALS

Agility trials began in the United Kingdom in 1977 and have since spread around the world, especially to the United States, where the sport enjoys strong popularity. The handler directs his dog over an obstacle course that includes jumps (such as those used in the working trials), as well as tyres, the dog walk, weave poles, pipe tunnels, collapsed tunnels, etc. The Kennel Club requires that dogs not be trained for agility until they are 12 months old. This dog sport intends to be great fun for dog and owner and interested owners should join a training club that has obstacles and experienced agility handlers who can introduce you and your dog

DID YOU KNOW?

The Kennel Club divides its dogs into seven Groups: Gundogs, Utility, Working, Toy, Terrier, Hounds and Pastoral.*

*The Pastoral Group, established in 1999, includes those sheepdog breeds previously categorised in the Working Group.

to the 'ropes' (and tyres, tunnels and so on).

FÉDÉRATION CYNOLOGIQUE INTERNATIONALE

Established in 1911, the Fédération Cynologique Internationale (FCI) represents the 'world kennel club.' This international body brings uniformity to the breeding, judging and showing of pure-bred dogs. Although the FCI originally included only five European nations: France, Holland, Austria, Germany and Belgium (which remains its headquarters), the organisation today embraces nations on six continents and recognises well over 300 breeds of purebred dog. There are three titles attainable through the FCI: the International Champion, which is the most prestigious; the International Beauty Champion, which is based on aptitude certificates in different countries; and the International Trial Champion, which is based on achievement in obedience trials in different countries. Dogs from every country can participate in these impressive FCI spectacles, the largest of which is the World Dog Show, hosted in a different country each year. FCI sponsors both national and international shows. The hosting country determines the judging system and breed standards are always based on the breed's country of origin.

INDEX

*Page numbers in **boldface** indicate illustrations.*

My Basset Hound

PUT YOUR PUPPY'S FIRST PICTURE HERE

Dog's Name _Daisy_

Date _____ Photographer _____